To Mary!
Blessings,
Billy Riddle

The Best to the Guest

Mama Polly in Liberia

POLLY RIDDLE

Inspiring Voices®

Copyright © 2014 Polly Riddle.

All rights reserved. No part of this book may be used or reproduced by any means, graphic, electronic, or mechanical, including photocopying, recording, taping or by any information storage retrieval system without the written permission of the publisher except in the case of brief quotations embodied in critical articles and reviews.

Inspiring Voices books may be ordered through booksellers or by contacting:

Inspiring Voices
1663 Liberty Drive
Bloomington, IN 47403
www.inspiringvoices.com
1 (866) 697-5313

Because of the dynamic nature of the Internet, any web addresses or links contained in this book may have changed since publication and may no longer be valid. The views expressed in this work are solely those of the author and do not necessarily reflect the views of the publisher, and the publisher hereby disclaims any responsibility for them.

Any people depicted in stock imagery provided by Thinkstock are models, and such images are being used for illustrative purposes only.
Certain stock imagery © Thinkstock.

ISBN: 978-1-4624-0978-5 (sc)
ISBN: 978-1-4624-0979-2 (e)

Library of Congress Control Number: 2014909004

Printed in the United States of America.

Inspiring Voices rev. date: 9/9/2014

Dedication

This diary of my trip to Liberia to teach adults would never have come about without the seeds sown by my mother, who in December of 2013 turned ninety-eight. When I was a child, she taught me elocution, generosity of spirit, perseverance, and the Bible. Her nurturing has returned a thousand-fold. Thank you, Mother.

In addition, I would like to dedicate this diary to the two women, Marinda and Martha, who took a chance on this American lady. Marinda knew me from her days at my church, and she knew I had helped her raise funds for her school. Martha knew me only as the teacher of math teachers and Frisbee player when our mission group came to her orphanage in 2010. Neither knew how I would react to their reality. Both were women in their fifties who had lost their husbands during the civil war in Liberia 1989-2004 and could have immigrated to the United States for a life of leisure. Instead, they sought to enrich their country with a school and an orphanage.

Finally, the diary is dedicated to the glory of God, who wishes all things well.

Preface

When Marinda Badio pursued her master's degree to become principal of a school being built in Monrovia, she attended Polly's church, St. Andrew's United Methodist. Polly secured money and books for the school.

In 2010 Polly went to see Marinda's school, Haweh Academy, and was asked to hand out kindergarten diplomas. Marinda had dubbed her "Mama Polly." In the courtyard after the graduation ceremony was a young man who looked to be fifteen. Mama Polly asked him if he was studying there or somewhere else. No? Then she asked, "What do you do?" He couldn't say.

Polly found out about the lost generation because of their conscription into the civil war (1989–2003) and other causes. They had no hope. When the war was over and the guns removed, they didn't know anything about making a living. Mama Polly was appalled: a young man without a positive future. She prayed.

After a bit, she realized she was being called to return to Liberia to teach a "Basics Boot-camp": two hours of phonics and literacy and one hour of arithmetic for twenty days. Her students would be men in the morning and women in the afternoon. She could give three months—one each in Monrovia, White Plains, and Ganta, each of which she had visited before. She was uniquely qualified for this at age sixty-eight, being a retired teacher of math and reading with a master's and a doctorate in English to speakers of other languages, plus a master's of divinity from a seminary. Her husband of more than thirty-seven years, Ira, had died in 2009, the year after they had moved to Ann's Choice, a senior living residence. Her home was protected.

She taught several adults from the community to read in Monrovia at Marinda's school. At Martha's orphanage in White Plains, she raised the skills of many adults; unfortunately, it was too close to Christmas, and possible students could not afford to take the time to come because they worked so hard for many hours. Since going to Ganta was not to be realized, she stayed in White Plains for three more weeks. She played phonics games, sang songs, danced, worshiped, led Bible studies, and exercised with the children.

The orphanage has a dream to produce cassava and other cash crops in order to build a library and a clinic on its grounds, which already includes a school. Now they want to start a Mama Polly-inspired night school that people could actually attend because they work during the day.

In Monrovia Mama Polly spent two extra weeks helping her former students, teaching two eleventh graders to upgrade their math background, and offering a literary Bible study on the gospel of Mark. This was to further the skills of her students and others. A Mama Polly night school is planned there, too. God was, and continues to be, in it all.

Acknowledgments

The many people of Inspiring Voices Publishing Company have made my diary come to life. I thank you.

My sister Carolyn proofread the diary twice and made suggestions. My friend and dinner companion Mary helped me proofread the semi-final product. Lee used his computer expertise to combine the separate parts. Marty, Howard, and Bill helped augment my computer skills. Many people have encouraged me by many different means. God be praised for all their efforts on my behalf.

Preparation: Summer 2011

To prepare for my adventure, I sought the counsel of Pastor Wendy at St. Andrew's UMC along with that of Jan and Beth of Compassion Corps. I had originally thought of leaving in May, but at an eye appointment in December, I was told to return to them in June for possible cataract surgery. I was also needed for a church mission trip to North Carolina in October. That would give me a chance to study at the School of Christian Mission in July as well as attend the Leadership Summit—and get my week at the beach in August. Finally, I decided that healing from surgery would be finished by the time I worked the election polls in November. Beth obtained plane tickets from Philadelphia to Monrovia via Atlanta and a visa for Saturday, November 12. The result of the eye exam was that I had cataracts, but they were not worth doing anything with them at that time.

Supplies for the mission came in dribbles. I told my friends at St. Andrew's I needed composition books, pens (both black and colored), markers, and pencils for 100 people. This number came to my head; I just didn't know how many students I would have. The provisions came in a timely manner to fill a barrel; the church sends three to four a year to Liberia, often to Marinda with school and church materials. One barrel would be dedicated for my trip. It was sent off in August so that it would arrive before me. People also gave me money since a missionary pays her own way. (Marinda uses the barrels to save rain water and however else her mind devises.)

In May, I attended the annual conference, the business part of church in eastern Pennsylvania. The Cokesbury Book Store was offering

$10 off if you spent $50. They had seeker New Testaments in a brand new translation, the Common English Bible (CEB), for $1.99 each. Since it was one coupon per person, I gathered three friends, and we each pre-ordered twenty-six to be sent at the beginning of September. I paid for mine and two others; one staked me for her box. The books arrived on time at each friend's home. One friend sent his to me; I went to the others' homes to collect them. That way I had 104 New Testaments to use as reading textbooks.

My friend Mary told me that a store was selling magnetic boards, so I bought two, each twenty-four by thirty-six inches. I also found easels at another store; since they were wrapped compactly, I trusted being able to put them together in Liberia. I bought books, posters, etc., from mail-order companies. The organist, Judie, gave me a garbage bag of freshly knit dolls from her friends to give out. I thanked her and wondered how I would pack them.

Since neither barrel nor suitcase was large enough for the boards, I went to a moving company and bought a cardboard box that was forty by forty by seven inches or so. I could barely get it into my car. At a hardware store, I bought casters for the box. Another friend, Gilda, whom I had taught to drive during the summer, installed the casters. We knew this oddly shaped box had to act like a suitcase at the airport.

Little by little, I was also completing my teaching curriculum. I needed to fill twenty days of instruction, which would get the students from beginner to second grade. At first, I put the lesson fragments on the backs of envelopes. I wrote the day (e.g., "Day 1") at the top and then numbered down one to ten for phonics and one to five for math. Number one was greetings, two was review, three was new material, four was a chart (mass learning), five was for writing something, six for sentence structure, seven for practice, eight for either eliciting sentences or a story from them, nine for new material, and ten for a passage from the CEB. It was like a horse race—some numbers got filled in, and other numbers came from behind. I wrote down my favorite Bible passages. If I liked them, the students would too, I figured. I had no regard for what I might be teaching on any given day. Finally, I typed and printed the plans.

The charts were put on a newsprint tablet. I bought a marker from the pharmacy and started writing. Since the marker bled onto the next page, I took a page I'd torn from my wall calendar and used it as a backing between each page. This also kept my printing straight. I had a gift for forming letters. As I wrote on the tablet, I showed the pages to Gilda, who is from the Philippines. She was overjoyed to see phonics and other structures written the way she would like to learn.

In September, Gilda and I made a *sandwich* on my bed: magnetic boards for the bread and 104 New Testaments for the filling. We wrapped five Ace bandages (they were on sale!) around the sandwich to keep the filling from falling out. She took one end and I took the other, and we went to the living room, where the box was lying on a card table. With plastic bubbles as a base, we shoved in the sandwich. The newsprint tablet went in on top. Then it was time for the posters and other flat items. In went my easels and the rolls of dry erase boards my friend Arlene had given me. We had a heavy box that was only half full. The knit dolls filled it to the brim! We closed up the box with two-inch tape. With masking tape bought in North Carolina, we finished securing the box; it had to get on the plane. We left it on the card table for two months, since we didn't trust the casters on the box to hold up for very long.

Soon it was time to get malaria pills. Unfortunately, my insurance allowed only for a one-month supply even though the doctor had specified eighteen pills, enough for three months. My phone call to the company assured me that they would override this dictum, but they didn't. When I got my pills at the pharmacy, their phone call resulted in being told that my insurance would cover only one month at a time. I paid full price for two extra months of pills, resulting in a total cost to me of $179. It is no wonder that I had not planned on getting malaria pills at all, but the people at Compassion Corps insisted.

In November, I started packing my duffel bag. I'd given it to the church for a project, but since they weren't using it, I stole it back. I was hoping to attend a preacher's seminar in Ganta, so I stuffed Bible study books to be distributed. Over the summer, Arlene and I had evaluated my blouses for possible use. I chose twelve to go into the bag. I also needed cotton skirts; Grace gave me a denim one she couldn't use. Late one November night, I entered a box store and asked for cotton skirts; the clerk brought three of different colors at $19.99 each. Sold—I bought them all! I'd tried earlier at a department store, but they had no skirts in cotton. The proverbial kitchen sink did not get into the body bag (as my sister called it), but it was full. It included my lesson plans with folders and three-by-five-inch flash cards for each day. I also threw in a thin towel, two wash rags, and a swimsuit (I never used the suit).

Friday, November 11, 2011

I went to borrow a cart from one of the Ann's Choice cart closets. I expected to have to use a grocery cart, but the flatbed carrier was there for my use. Wonderful! Gilda and I gently eased the box to the cart so that it would stand on its side. We put the bag next to it and left it overnight.

Saturday, November 12, 2011

Tim, a friend from the church, had volunteered to take me to the airport. I wheeled the cart to the elevator and pushed it outside. While he put the bag and box into his van, I returned the cart. Off we went at noon!

At the Philadelphia airport, I was able to wheel the box and bag through the check-in line. The clerk told me they were too heavy and oversized. Imagine that! She told me the price, which I barely heard, and I handed her a charge card. Box and bag were now accepted as luggage. I chased down a postal box and sent the receipt to the church. They paid it with discretionary funds.

At 3:30 p.m., the plane headed for Atlanta. By 9:15 that night, I was aboard the plane to Monrovia. Gratefully, there was nothing remarkable about the flight. I read, slept, and ate.

Sunday, November 13, 2011

I arrived at the Monrovia airport at 4:25 p.m., as scheduled. This Delta flight took us first to Accra, Ghana, where we did not get off but saw the workers clean the plane. Monrovia is five hours ahead of the East Coast.

My blue bag, with a *heavy* tag attached to it, came off the conveyer belt. The box, stripped of its casters, was brought in. I claimed it right away. A zealous sky cap took charge and put them on a cart. I lost the luggage tags in my purse when I was looking for tip money. When the sky cap found out I was a missionary, he persuaded the customs officials that I was okay. At least my name was on the bag and box; I did not want to unpack either one.

Marinda, her vice principal, and her son James (as opposed to John, who works for President Sirleaf) took over as I left the airport and got my bags in the car. James drove. The main airport road was nicely paved, but we turned onto another road that was less so. The New Georgia Road was rutty. Then we took the squirrel trails that led to Marinda's school, Haweh Academy, and her home. As always, *Slow and steady wins the race.*

Along the way, we had gotten food prepared by her caterer daughter, Marie—flavored rice, potato salad, and chicken. I enjoyed bottled water while Marinda fixed herself Ovaltine. It was hard to sort out the people who lived at Marinda's home. Face recognition is not my forte.

After dinner, Marinda and I moved to the bedroom, where I unpacked the box, bag, and barrel sent earlier. She marveled at the curriculum I'd devised. Supplies got spread out onto tables, shelves, and into cabinets, both hers and mine.

Monday, November 14, 2011

When I left my room to see if I could help in any way, Marinda's family was busy cleaning the common areas. Her daughter Genevieve lives in the house with her husband, Charles Alpha, and two children, Denise, age eight, and Charles Jr., age two. Two high school girls, Otally and Cristie, live in another bedroom and help clean and cook. Three high school boys (Marcus, Abbis, and Josephus) live in a room at the school and do sweeping and water-hauling chores. When I realized I would be in the way if I came to breakfast too early (a guest does no work), I returned to my room for my morning devotions and diary writing. Marinda had given up her room so that I could have privacy and her private toilet, for which I was most grateful. I think she slept with the girls.

During the school day, Marinda first took me around to meet the students and their teachers in their classrooms. Then I settled in a room where I put address labels on my late husband, Ira's, magnet-backed business cards—two each of *ad, an, at, am,* and the other vowels with these consonants, and also of *b, g, ck,* and *p*. We'd use them on the magnetic boards I'd brought in the big box. On the backing of the label sheets, I put useful phrases like *God is good—All the time; Love the Lord your God with all your heart, mind, and soul (being); Love your neighbor as yourself;* and *Now abide faith, hope, and love, but the greatest of these is love.*

A father of six children at the school, John McIntosh, came in to chat while I was working with the magnets. He worked at Scripture Union, an organization dedicated to encouraging the reading of the Bible, and was interested in replicating what I was doing. Since I was working with my husband's old business cards, I told him about the death of my husband. It had been just over two years that he had died suddenly while on a cruise ship in France. It was easier to have his ashes returned to me rather than his body. John and I compared Liberian funerals with the cremations of Ira and my father. Liberia does not have many crematoriums.

At the end of the school day, I was honored in an assembly At the assembly Marinda told the students how "Mama Polly," as she called me, had helped raise a lot of money for their school while she (Marinda) was in the United States getting her degree in "Principalship." Marinda had attended my church during the two years she was studying. I brought them greetings from everyone in the United States, especially those in my home town. Piggy-backing on what someone had said earlier in the assembly about being afraid, I encouraged the students to get an idea and run with it, even though they might be fearful.

After lunch—plain rice and potato greens with chicken—I put together my two easels. They'd work, but barely. The newsprint tablet would be tried the next day. I read the introduction of 1 Thessalonians in my Spanish commentary.

Marinda and I took a walk with a few others around New Georgia Old Field. We saw dust on the path, homes that looked good or ramshackle, people selling, and lots of motorcycles. Marinda's house has no plumbing, except perhaps the toilet, which is emptied with water poured into it. The water was pumped from the well on the property. Electricity had come only recently to the edge of the 'burb. It would take a while to get it to the school. The house was lit by a loud, smelly, fickle generator and candles. Food was cooked on braziers outside. The flashlights and lanterns ran on batteries.

Day 1: Tuesday, November 15

I started teaching both classes today. Three men came not to learn the information but to see how I presented it. Actually, they were learning the phonics I was teaching, and some of the vocabulary (tot, tat, tam, nit) was new to them. They wanted me to write the "next step" curriculum, too. The morning was so chaotic that instead of having classes from nine in the morning to noon, we went from ten thirty to one and just did phonics. I got lots of water at lunch and was ready to go again by two.

It was raining at that point, but six women arrived at two forty-five. Later, three more women straggled in. The women were apt students and were happy to be learning. I was happy to be teaching. The first day's lesson involved *a, t, d, m, n*. We made lots of words from that combination. Near the end of the lesson, I introduced the circle as *o* and the short line as *i* and used them in syllables and words. The students had made circles and lines on the backs of envelopes I'd brought to practice forming letters.

I was served a VIP dinner of rice and black-eyed peas. I told Marinda that the same dinner was served in the South on New Year's Day. I was given a chair at the table in front of Marinda but no one else was at the table. A blank yellow wall was behind her; I was rarely aware of anyone behind me in the living room as I ate. I went to bed early.

Day 2: Wednesday, November 16

The three men came to classes again, but another man came who actually needed my services, Nathaniel. Gratefully, he came first, and I caught him up with the rest of the class. The others helped him pick up the slack. We learned eleven more consonants and the other two vowels. I even got the math in, including odd/even, greater than/less than, and ordinal/cardinal numerals from 1–10.

The women were to come at two o'clock, but Martha, who would host me at the orphanage in White Plains, came to get a better schedule of my events. Since they had waited patiently last year while the group met President Sirleaf, I figured my women could wait a few minutes. It's called Liberian time. I still eventually had eight women students today, including two new ones. One of them needed to catch up. She hadn't helped herself by coming in late.

Marinda's generator was run by gasoline, which is expensive at US $4.50 a gallon. After it was turned off or fizzled out, I read using a battery-operated affair given to me by Marinda. In the morning, I found myself getting up when I was able to see my hand in the air. I could put up the mosquito netting, make the bed, and go into the bathroom by natural light. By the time I had washed myself and my clothes, the sun would be streaming behind the palm trees enough for me to write in my diary and have my devotions. I learned to stay in my room until I was called to breakfast, which was usually cream of wheat.

Day 3: Thursday, November 17

This morning Nathaniel came early, so I began teaching early. He needed to learn to form his letters starting with *a*. He must have been a carpenter, because he could handle a ruler as a straight edge. Only *e* was difficult for him to form. We then got to consonant blends. Once he learned the vowel names, he could read my phonetically formed words. Such a breakthrough!

The afternoon class started late, but it was also one for effective review. The woman student I wanted to help did not come until five o'clock, at the end of the school day, but I vowed to help her whenever she came.

I also got the attendance sheet, so I could call the people by name. It is fun asking questions from Luke 10, the story of the good Samaritan. They are learning well.

Day 4: Friday, November 18

Nathaniel returned for more learning. John was absent; he probably had to work at his job at the Christian Scripture Union. Later in the morning a new man came to learn phonics. Some students knew the alphabet but not the structure of the language. English is their native language, and I'm giving them the building blocks for reading (i.e. short and long vowels with the first hundred common words; *man shall not read by phonics alone!*). What I taught today, syllabification of *cle* words (consonant + *le:* am / ple) was used to help read Acts 3:1–8 with the words *cripple, temple, ankle*. Only God could form a lesson plan three months in advance to engineer this. I'd taught long *a* (*ai*), and in the story were the words *raised* and *praising*.

In the afternoon, two new women came, but some of the others didn't. One came even though she was sick. I had put the second day's reading on the wall. Both classes had people who could now read it, though they couldn't have at first on Day 2.

A friend from my church had given me roll-up dry erase boards. I used part of one to put the Good Samaritan story in permanent ink. The story stayed up for all twenty days.

After dinner we got out Marinda's laptop. She needed help in getting her server. I hope my message to Ellen, who would forward it to others, really got sent. After the noisy generator came on, we had light, and I could read a little. (I later learned that no e-mails ever got through.)

Day 5: Saturday, November 19

We had a combined class of men and women today: one man and four women. We still put in three hours, writing *v, w, x, y, z, j*; using prepositions (writing them in blue on the Good Samaritan story); working with the long *i* (-igh, -y); and practicing numbers by tens and place value. We helped the one student who didn't know how to subtract.

Marinda served "dumb-boy" for lunch: cooked dough from cassava with okra, eggplant, chicken, fish, and broth. The broth made from the palava plant turned the big dumpling into exquisite fare. It's a favorite of Liberians, so I may have it again.

In the afternoon, Marinda, Marcus, and I went to give medical supplies to the clinic, but it had closed and moved to another place. We then took a cab Liberia-style: we three got in the car, and soon two more got in.

We went to the shopping center nearby. First I stopped at the Internet café, where I checked my e-mails and deleted most of them. I sent another e-mail to Ellen. Then we shopped at a grocery store, which had a guard at both the entrance and exit. The owner/cashier stood tall at the front collecting money. Clerks wore green T-shirts; I saw five of them in a place no bigger that St. Andrew's UMC sanctuary. There were four aisles with cans and packages neatly stacked. We stopped at the bulk flour and rice store, but I don't remember what was bought. Marinda was in charge of the refreshments for the ladies' aid installation of officers. I'm to install them.

We took another cab going back along New Georgia Road; Marcus carried the heavy items, Marinda the lighter ones, and I got to carry one bag as we finished our journey by walking home for ten or fifteen minutes. Homes are made of concrete blocks, bamboo sheets, or whatever. A once-beautiful home was destroyed in the war. It had exquisite remnants but was a mere shell of a building. I saw many abandoned homes like this.

Sunday, November 20

There was a huge storm here last night. The lightning flashed. I heard the booms. The bedroom and bathroom doors slammed shut in the wind. The rain came onto the bed sideways through the slats. I closed the jalousie windows, but two panes were missing. This morning I stripped the newly made bed, putting sheets on the barrels and the partly-sopped blanket over the headboard. The pillow that bore the brunt of the rain would need direct sun. I was glad the far side of the bed stayed dry. I was able to sleep.

The pillow dried well on the car outside. Much of the laundry was often put on all sides of the car to dry. Heavy pants were put on the five-foot-high concrete wall around the school/house compound. The biggest wash day was Saturday; if the laundry wasn't taken down before dusk but left overnight, it would be soaked.

I was accorded honor at church and moved to the chancel area to sit. This means that I could hear very little, since everyone's back was to me. I was asked to give the benediction, and I did. The preacher, Pastor Charles Alpha, who is married to Marinda's daughter Genevieve, preached on the question, "How do you see yourself?" At Bible study on the previous Wednesday evening, I had given a testimony of how, during my ordination process, people had asked that question. I answered, "As a bridge." I am a bridge to the Liberian people and their continued education.

While others in the house cleaned up after the storm, I was a guest and not allowed to help. I got to sit at the table while others either ate in their rooms or, this day, ate together on the chairs of the living room. I felt other.

The installation of officers for the Haweh Academy Mothers' Prayer Fellowship was scheduled for three o'clock today. Since the president didn't arrive on time, we waited and began at four; after all, we were on Liberian time. We opened with "O Come All Ye Faithful." The choir sang beautifully, after which came a skit, "Let Jesus Put Your Heavy Burden Down." I was the installer and gave each office a name from the Bible: President, Priscilla; VP, Naomi; Treasurer, Lydia; Secretary, the Virtuous Woman of Proverbs 31; Contact person, Dorcas; Prayer Coordinator, Hannah. It was well received. After some remarks, we had refreshments: a can or bottle of soda and a sandwich made of two slices of white bread with a thin meat spread inside. It was brought to us.

Day 6: Monday, November 21

Marinda served oatmeal instead of her preferred cream of wheat this morning. She also had freshly made cruller doughnuts. At her insistence, I ate a second one.

Nathaniel came, and we began with long *o*, the two *oo* sounds, *oy*, and *oi*. This was ambitious, but I had it on one board, which I also saved to use with the women. On the other board, I put cards with consonant digraphs (*sh, th, ph, wh, ch*). I tried to save that too, but the newsprint tablet smeared them all around.

John of Scripture Union was interested in how I teach and my American dialect. Today he noticed how the *e* changes before a vowel sound (the r̲oad, versus the i̲njured or the o̲ther). I got carried away giving my slant of the Good Samaritan story. At least we had time for the "Feeding of the Five Thousand" (Mark 6:30–44).

In the women's class, hard as it was, we slugged through the *o* lessons. Women kept coming. I rejoiced when there were ten in class, the most we'd had. One more came. Two who had pre-registered finally showed up. Consistency of attendance for many is not in their make-up. They also get sick, have sick kids, and deal with home chores.

Conjunctions were next. I had written clauses like "the women went to worship" and "the men stayed home." For many, that was life on Sunday afternoon, so it was relevant. I heard some titters of laughter as we went through each conjunction to illustrate dependent and independent clauses. What fun and ridiculousness!

We read our "Feeding of the Five Thousand." In any of these passages, I first read the story slowly. I would stop to talk about what we'd read and ask questions. This gave the students time to reflect on the words themselves and the concepts. Today I gave them "advanced organizers" of the phonics of the day (feed, green, sheep, loaves). Some just looked at me, and others took it all in. For the second reading, we read together without stopping, hopefully.

In the math part, we reviewed and started multiplication and division. At the end of thirty minutes, I asked who needed help in subtraction, especially borrowing. This was their time; those who didn't need help could copy something or leave. No one left, but three got "borrowing." Some copied or just enjoyed being. I was gratified. They all wanted to help bring my things to the office, but I needed to straighten out my own mess. One student stayed and let me do things at my pace. Then I could delegate. Others learned to do this, too.

Polly Riddle

Each day we have rice and a delicious combo of chicken and vegetable for dinner. Today, after our meal, one of Marinda's teachers came. He'd just buried his forty-nine-year-old mother, who'd had a stroke. The two of us prayed for him. I gave him a composition book, pen, and New Testament so that he could write about his feelings. He didn't seem to have a friend yet. He could read how Jesus suffered and use the suggestions at the beginning of the book that showed the passages for grief. My seminary training had kicked in.

Day 7: Tuesday, November 22

Today is the anniversary of President Kennedy's death.

I had everyone draw a dog and tell what it did best. Then we described the dog (size, color, fur type). Nathaniel's dog was completely different from Samuel's. Then we compared how, when, where, and to what extent the dogs did their thing (run, guard, bark, jog, wag tails). Suddenly we were talking about adjectives and adverbs. Nathaniel in the morning and some women in the afternoon could read my adjective opposites without me. They recognized they were reading, using all the clues they'd had. Glory be to God!

Mamie (pronounced *Mah-mee*) in the afternoon read with me in the first reading about Jesus's walk on water in the storm (Matthew 6:45–52). She led the class in the second reading. They'd transferred their learning to get "secluded, isolated, and struggling." How God-inspired these lesson plans were!

Day 8: Wednesday, November 23

Nathaniel knows how to multiply, so I decided to try guessing and thinking games with him. Paul and his shipwreck (Acts 27:27–44) was too long, with too many unknown concepts. I tried to help by outlining it with the women, but it was either too dark in the room or too complicated. Nathaniel could sound out the words, but he had no comprehension.

We had eleven women in class today, who all arrived at different times. They like to copy things, even when I want to teach something else. It is heartrending to me to snatch a poster away. We learned to laugh when I turned a board to its back. They realized I wanted their attention on me for more instruction, not the board for copying.

At night we went to Bible study. How did the Israelites see themselves when they were spies (Numbers 13:33)? As grasshoppers. There was no electricity, just a few flashlights. Marinda's generator had been on the fritz, even with a new part.

Day 9: Thursday, November 24

Today was Thanksgiving in the United States. Liberians celebrate Thanksgiving earlier in the month.

Both Nathaniel and John were late, but when they did make it in, they came within five minutes of each other. We did *r*- and *w*-controlled vowels in the morning class, plus the house chart, and then started reading "The Shipwreck" (Acts 27) verse by verse. We explained words and got an idea of all the details and main ideas: sailors, soldiers, Paul and other prisoners, and how they all landed safely. John thought about the story each of these men would tell their family and friends when they got home or back to the garrison. I hadn't thought of it as a way to spread the story, either. God surely has a sense of humor.

The women also enjoyed the Acts 27 shipwreck story, and we read and explained it verse by verse. They wanted to know why Paul was a prisoner and where he was going. I gave them an analogy: "*Centurion* is to *soldiers* as *captain* is to *sailors*." We did all of the morning lessons and also got to multiplication and division by 2 and 3. After class some of the women swept the dust from the classroom. They bent low to use the crude broom they had.

After a dinner of beans and rice, Marinda, Marcus (a ward), and I went to the internet café, a ten- or fifteen- minute walk through the dusty, rutted neighborhood. It took an hour for me to delete ninety messages and send two e-mails. The "n" key was sticking. A handy flashlight lit our way once the newly installed lights of Old Georgia Road were a memory. Progress came slowly.

Day 10: Friday, November 25

I was putting cards on the boards and trying to anchor them when Nathaniel came in. Rather than have him wait, I brought the board over to him. We studied soft *g* and *c* words that way. I got them anchored for the women. Nathaniel and I then went to adjectives with *y* to add *-er* and *-est*. It was fun to read Acts 9, Paul's conversion, with him and John. The three of us alternated verses.

The women came in as usual and got the above lessons as well. Math included diagonals and the thought of finding half of an area, which is dividing by 2. This was new ground. We then multiplied and divided by 4, 5, and 6. Only one could do it by herself.

After a short dinnertime, since Marinda had gone to town, I went with Marcus to the internet café to send one e-mail. The e-mail was sent in due season; it was still slow. Marcus let me walk quickly along the rutty lanes and beside the road. On the way back, I tripped over a small root that I should have seen. *Splat!* I got up with Marcus's help, but he was devastated. He should have prevented such a thing. Back at the house, we washed the bruise on my arm with none-too-sterile water, dried it with a used bath towel, put hand sanitizer on it, applied Neosporin, and put two Band-Aids on it. Since the area was still wet, the Band-Aids came off after a time, but Marcus, the guardian responsible for my well-being, was absolved of guilt. Alone, I might have done differently. I thank God there were no ill effects. I put a pillow under my legs and kept them on the sofa for the rest of the evening while we watched a video; my pillow was also under my knees in bed. (Four weeks later, I tried to show my scar to someone at the orphanage but couldn't find it.)

Saturday, November 26

After staying up past my bedtime, I woke up late. So did everyone else. Actually, I'd been the party pooper and the first one to leave the night before; the rest of the family watched more movies. This was wash day and change sheets day. I had some interesting small sheets put on my double bed, but they worked.

Tage Swallie, Director of Healthline Medical Clinic at Lifeline Network, Liberia, owned a clinic, which he operated in a rental building from 2003 to 2011 in New Georgia Township (I saw this on my first visit in 2010). Tage had since moved to Barnersville. He, Marinda, and I walked to the old clinic, where people were still being helped. We met Tage's wife, who is a midwife. We again viewed the rooms: uptake, doctor's office, lab, men's stay room, women's stay room, maternity delivery, and pharmacy. The waiting area was on the roofed porch outside.

The three of us were driven to the new clinic, a recently built edifice that will serve an area poorer than the current one. Those in Old Field New Georgia had other clinics to choose from. Commerce along the road was brisk, with small stalls among larger buildings. Ambulatory vendors sold items from baskets on their heads or in wheelbarrows. I also saw schools, clinics, churches, and political entities. There had been an election on the November 8, as we had in the United States. A sign said, "Stick with Ellie and Joe." (President Ellen Sirleaf and Vice President Joseph N. Boakai were re-elected.)

We turned left onto a paved road, but soon the paving ended and we ended up on a one-lane set of ruts. At the end was the new clinic. The same kinds of rooms were there, only bigger. There was also a room for the administrator. Tage's daughter would graduate as a nurse in December. Her fiancé would graduate early next summer in sociology and would be in administration. The driver taking us to the clinic was actually a pastor and electrician in the area. We saw his church. Together they hope someday to build a school. Barnersville will grow and need more than they have now.

We also saw Tage's house. Their former garage was now a pharmacy. They had delivered three hundred babies at the house. For the clinic, they needed any equipment any medical entity wants to cast off, and the dream was to get an ambulance. We met the doctor-assistant; I never heard anyone say there was a full doctor around.

The beauty of Liberia could be seen in the plants in front of the house. Tage will be able to walk to work. In answer to my question, "Are you better off now or before the war?" the driver/pastor/electrician said he didn't have a car before the war and now he does. A rising tide lifts all boats. Now all Liberians have access to a boat.

Sunday, November 27

The sun rose outside my window behind the palm trees. I saw the bustle of people, mostly children, coming to the pump in the school yard to the best water in the neighborhood. They took their places in line and helped one another. The sunlight helped me read.

I got dressed in my green two-piece dress I'd bought at Corina Hotel in Monrovia in 2010 and went with Marinda to the Lighthouse Baptist Church, just off Tubman Boulevard, a thirty-minute cab ride away. It was a good walk past the Corina Hotel. We arrived in time for Sunday school. The speaker, who later would preach, spoke on life not only being a journey and a circle, but also a test and a trust. God gives us lessons we need to learn, and we will be faced with similar problems until we learn them. We were entrusted to act for God in service to nature, mankind, and God. After all, we are God's hands and feet.

The church service had three hymns I knew from a hymn book, sung *very* slowly. The lively native hymns were sung and danced with drums and native bell shakers. I was asked to say a few words about why I was there. Pastor John Ndorbor, whom in 2010 I had seen ordained and anointed to be head pastor of the church, recognized me; he would speak at my church in Warminster the next February. Marinda spoke as a first-time visitor.

Pastor John told the story of how David returned to Ziklag (1 Samuel 30:1–18) and found that the Amalekites had taken away their belongings and families. David was distressed, but he prayed. Then he led his men to get them back. Along the way, they helped a man who led them to where the enemy had gone. It pays to help people. I didn't catch everything; the rain was pelting on the tin roof in this not-so-dry season. The service ended at 1:15. The taxi was to return at 1:30 and did so at 2:45. I was glad someone offered me a bathroom as well as a soda.

At 5:30 the rains came again. Unusual weather! Showers of blessing.

Day 11: Monday, November 28

I had put the story of the Good Samaritan on my dry erase roll in permanent marker. Previously, we had marked prepositional phrases in blue parentheses. Today we underlined subjects once and verbs twice in red. The students also copied my Basic Sentence Structure chart (Subject–Predicate; Subject–Predicate Nominative or Adjective). We had a predicate nominative in the story: "one was neighbor."

One woman came in just as we finished. I helped her add in two digits while the rest of the class was doing multiplication and division. This latter they do well *with* me, but not by themselves. In the morning, Nathaniel read for Marinda, who gave him twenty LD (Liberian dollars), about five US dollars, for his achievement.

Marinda served me crackers from the fancy package and cheese wedges, a typical lunch for me, and then she hot-footed it to the Department of Ministry of Education to renew and update her Haweh Academy High School certificate.

I'd told her what I ate for lunch at home, and she tried to replicate it here, even though I've told her I wanted the Liberian rice. For her it is so humble. For me it is real food, and I'm missing it. I again told the daughter that I like to experiment with a country's rice and beans. I told them of my mission trips to Spanish-speaking countries. At dinner, I was served white bread sandwiches with thinly applied tinned meat filling—all very fancy. I prefer 100 percent whole wheat bread.

Marinda came back excited to show her letter extending her permit. The fancy certificate will follow. Liberians are quite capable of gobbledygook, as the letter showed.

Tuesday, November 29

Today is a holiday, as it is former President William Tubman's birthday. I took a picture of the sun behind the palm trees. I told daughter Genevieve that I wake up in paradise each day in Liberia. It's beautiful. She thanked me.

We were supposed to learn about square dancing, with myself as the caller and teacher. Marinda got so bogged down with school officials with ledgers in hand that there was no time for dancing. I kept three-year-old Charles, Jr., away from another three-year-old, a girl, but the *Reader's Digest* I was reading excited him too much. I got out my Flip Book, a picture book of items. Junior liked it. Turnabout is fair play—it was enticing to the girl, too, of course. One can't win.

Marinda fed us rice with chicken and eggplant. Yum! I overdosed on it and couldn't eat the cake she made.

At two o'clock, she and I set out for a fundraiser for Angie, a pastor at Alliance Church. She had recorded a professional album and needed support for her undertaking. It was another example of Liberians helping Liberians, since it was held at Doe Juah UMC, just past the internet café. We could have walked, but Marinda wanted to be fresh, so she hailed a cab.

This fundraiser was like a spirited church service—lots of prayer for Angie and her church and lots of praises sung to God. Mostly women sang for us. As they sang, people danced up to the big bucket and threw money in it. Sometimes money was stuffed in Angie's dress or just tossed in her vicinity. The UMC minister, sitting facing the audience, threw money toward the bucket. Marinda was a sponsor, and when she was allowed to speak, she told the congregation what I was doing: bringing supplies and teaching for free. I brought greetings from Pastor Wendy in the United States and said I was trying to spread scriptural holiness (a theme of John Wesley) and reading through the land. I told the "in Jesus's name" story of my Muslim friend who wanted me to pray for a baby. When I visited her next, she'd had three children "in Jesus's name."

When we left the fundraiser, the assistant principal of Haweh Academy, who wore a T-shirt from Angie's church, walked us to a place where we could cross the road safely. He returned to the church, and we started our way home. The internet café was busy, so we went on. We bought oranges and bananas at separate stands. Marinda picked up some grain she had bought. We walked home, waving and greeting people we knew. I didn't hear them, but Marinda did. The dog at the compound greeted Marinda profusely and tore a hole in her grain bag. After some came loose, she gathered the bag in her skirt. Others went for a bowl to catch the grain. I offered one of the bags from the bananas. Junior tried to help too, but someone ushered him away. Life goes on.

I got the cake for dinner and a banana. I was full. Marinda and I talked. She called Jan Bean from Compassion Corps and my sister. No one was home, so we left messages.

Day 12: Wednesday, November 30

We started the affix (prefix/suffix) and stem/root chart and created words with *form, tolerate,* and *author.* Zacchaeus was saved and returned as a "son of Abraham" (Luke 19:1–10). Most of the translations say "Son of Man," but this new CEB says "the Human One." We had another day of division. In the afternoon, the women did a lot during a rainstorm; we could barely see and hear one another. Our skylight ceiling was dim.

The prayer meeting after dinner—yam greens and chicken over rice—was full of singing and praise to God. We were anointed for service. I went up and laid my hands on the preachers, returning the blessing to them. It was unplanned. I am thankful and give praise to God that my skinned arm is healing well, the people are learning, the household is healthy and harmonious, and the sunrise is so romantic each morning.

Polly Riddle

Day 13: Thursday, December 1

Mamie brought a whole bowl of bananas. She's brought other fruit in appreciation of my teaching her to read.

Today was World AIDS Day. Testing and antiviral drugs were given free to people who were HIV infected, since 85 percent of Liberian women are HIV or AIDS positive. Men, as a rule, do not come for testing. There was an assembly about it for the kids. I got all this info in the morning.

That morning at school, the teacher whose mother had died suddenly came by to say the New Testament, pen, and composition book I had given him really worked wonders. He was at much greater peace now.

At the assembly, the music was loud. I danced to it a bit while Nathaniel wrote. It was too loud to teach, but we persevered. I gave him some fractions and third-grade logic problems about digits. In both classes, we did *ough* words (offering hints at how they were pronounced), *-ject* and *-scribe/script* affixes, and the denial of Peter (Luke 22:54–65). It was fun to stare at someone, as the woman did to Peter. It was good to list the *who* and *when* of the cause of Peter's failure.

In the evening, after pea stew and chicken over rice, Marinda and I made a condolence call to a woman whose nineteen-year-old son had drowned in the ocean; he was a brother of a student at Haweh Academy. Marinda is big on caring. I prayed at the end.

We talked about money needs for Liberians: a generator for Mama Polly Night School was $1,500 and includes backup; Pre-kindergarten to kindergarten fees were $150 per year; 1–6 grades were $10 more each grade; high school was more; and University of Liberia for a three-trimester year was $500.

Day 14: Friday, December 2

I went on record to say I would pay for the generator out of my income tax refund. The old one was four years old and needed to be repaired more often than it worked.

The Best to the Guest

I gave Nathaniel the steps to the Business CreAction (create and act) Plan. He liked that. We'll see what he comes up with for himself. He's smart but has a limited fund of concepts. I wish I had more picture books to explain things. The women are more savvy.

Eight women dragged themselves in for *i before e*—receive vs. relieve—and transportation items. I had planned ten words, but this group was driving me to create a whole tablet sheet of concepts. No one, including Nathaniel, had studied fractions, decimals, and per cents. We would spend a few days with them, as they were part of my extended curriculum. The women got multiplication and division on their own when I showed them how to use the nice table in their composition books.

Day 15: Saturday, December 3

We held a Saturday session to make up for the holiday. From nine to noon, we had a joint session of men and women. Nathaniel came first, then John and a couple of women. More dribbled in until there were nine women and two men. We learned the *-vent* and *-mit* words, regular verbs—which made a good phonics review—and more about fractions. I blew their minds when I introduced decimals: .1 = .10!

In the afternoon, I taught some square dancing moves to a few of Marinda's students. I thought we'd be in the hot sun on the concrete slab of the courtyard, but thankfully we were in the auditorium/sanctuary. Some moves I couldn't teach, even though I could execute them well at Ann's Choice, the senior center where I live. I'm dependent on knowledgeable men when it comes to square dancing.

For a late lunch and dinner, I ate *palava*, a plant that grows a bit tall and has long, skinny leaves in triplet formation. It is made into a topping for *fufu* (foofoo), a big dumpling made of cassava. It could be stuffed with chicken or other meat. The combo was delicious. By itself the fufu was doughy.

At night I met some of Marinda's family. They enjoyed learning La Raspa, a dance of Spanish origin, and the Bunny Hop, a teen dance of the 1950s, to the tune of the hymn "Lord of the Dance." It was enjoyable to make fools of ourselves under the shining half moon. We did not need other light outside.

Sunday, December 4

After walking the dusty warrens to New Georgia Road on the way to church, Marinda and I got into a cab that was already full and were the first to get out. We attended the New Georgia UMC, arriving while the choir was singing for this first Sunday of Advent. My right hearing aid battery failed, so my left aid allowed for limited understanding. I missed the African beat of the Christmas carols; that is, I heard the beat but did not recognize the songs and did not get to sing them. I understood perfectly, however, the sermon on Mark 8:1—*repent!* Youth joined the church that Sunday. I was introduced by Marinda and was asked to speak. Later a woman from Sweden spoke; she was interested in Sunday schools in general, but especially of the churches built and rebuilt after the Liberian civil war. NGUMC was built in 1992, during the war. Its motto is: "The church with a vision and the vision at work." Pastor Wendy has met the pastor.

It being the first Sunday of the month, we had communion. The pastor held out a wafer, and I took it. I guess for others it was put directly into the mouth. One was to eat it quickly, receive the communion cup, drink from it, and put the cup into the handy basin supplied. A woman supplied the pastor with more wafers, the deacon with more communion cups, and another basin-holder another basin. It was a well-oiled way to proceed. People were directed from the back to the front. One woman gave me a lace doily for my head. Another retrieved it after I'd communed. I had missed how it should be returned. One must not go uncovered to communion if a woman.

Going home, we again got into an already full cab. The driver would get money for the distance we rode. Back home, the kidney beans and chicken over rice were waiting for us. The others in the household had eaten or were just finishing.

I went with Marinda to her office on the second floor atop the sanctuary. She had a corner office and could see students in the courtyard. The administrator who handled money had a small room next door. When time and money permit, the private toilet and sink room could be finished. I sat on the padded sofa and read while she graded papers. Later, she and Samuel, the youth minister and choir director, talked over plans for their teen camp between Christmas and New Year. Topics at the camp would include sexual purity and what's not, drugs, forgiving yourself, and integrity. She liked my definition of this last—doing right when no one is looking. It's not really my definition.

After dinner—spicy potato greens with crawfish over rice—we sang the carols of her Christmas play. Abbis and Marcus joined in. I remembered "The Twelve Days of Christmas" and taught it. Rollicking!

Day 16: Monday, December 5

I finally realized part of Nathaniel's comprehension problem was his inability to see the words. If my old glasses fit, he'll get them. He loved my new reading glasses. They will help his far vision also. We studied the walk to Emmaus, community places (my original ten being expanded to three columns), and *-tain* and *port*. Then we combined the sentences: "We walked on the grass," "The grass is green," and "We met Jane." Another set of sentences: "A man is named Zack." "He is a ruler." "He is rich." What fun to put them with conjunctions, *wh-* words, and past participles! The CEB uses these constructions to the hilt. We worked with the 4 operations of fractions and a quick overview of decimals. The intention was to introduce it all. I didn't expect them to master it. It was amazing what they were able to learn so quickly, though.

The night sky at the equator (we were five degrees north) is a marvel. Marcus said that what I thought were stars were really satellites.

Day 17: Tuesday, December 6

Nathaniel got my glasses and could copy better from the board. When we read scripture, Jesus and the ten, then eleven, from John 20, he read well and without trouble, even wanting to read on. They are his glasses now. May they be used for God's glory.

My two smart ladies, Rebecca and Tenneh, came early, and I let them copy what they didn't get to at the beginning: pronouns and verb *to be*. Mamie came in; she'd learned to read also. I let them copy the "One-Minute CreAction Plan" after discussing it. A new woman Evelyn copied it, too. As it turns out, when I asked them their dreams, they wanted to be in business: two as seamstress, to travel, international business. All have been uplifted. Then they asked what my dreams were. I told them, after I wrote on the board that I wanted to cry, about ministry, being a bridge, and being willing and able to follow God's lead. I was doing that dream; it was moving to us all.

Day 18: Wednesday, December 7

The new man, Morris Taylor, an observer from Scripture Union, copied my early charts. John was kept busy watching us all. Nathaniel copied the clothing and occupation words, irregular plurals, and modals. We had quite a discussion with it all. John's minister came in and heard me expound on Peter's reinstatement (John 21:1–14). Math was division of decimals, which was easy for Nathaniel.

The women copied faster and with more comprehension, as usual. My back was sore, so Tina gave me some manipulations. She can't read, as she came in late most of the time, but she surely can massage. Some of the women are getting division, but math is a struggle. Sexism wins.

After dinner of pea stew with chicken over rice, we went to Bible study. We learned about being frauds at communion. Since "everybody knows" how to do communion, no directions were given. I did it differently, of course. Marinda said she was caught her first time, too.

I thought it was my lack of hearing. Outside there was almost a full moon, which was great for talking in the cool of the evening, even with the bugs around. My white skin invited mosquitoes.

Day 19: Thursday, December 8

Today, my twin grand-nieces had their third birthday back in the States.

Morris came early to write more from my newsprint tablet. I would explain it and then let him write. He finally said that everything would be lifeless without Mama Polly behind it. He asked if I could write a lesson book to explain exactly what I did, how, and why I did it. It would be used throughout Liberia and perhaps other places in Africa. I finally realized I *could* write it and would try to take good notes while I was in White Plains and Ganta. The Lord has blessed the work here exceedingly! (After finishing a draft of this diary when I returned to the United States, the lesson book was completed.)

Nathaniel came, and I proceeded to two-word coordinating conjunctions: "not only, but also" and "neither, nor." The irregular verbs that I thought would take two days took only thirty minutes. Copying was quick for those who had learned, the women too. I've learned to deal with their staggered entrances; the smart ones, though, come on time.

After dinner of eggplant and chicken over rice (we had some papaya—*paw paw*—for lunch with bread and cheese), Marinda and I went walking to the revival service I'd been invited to by some of my students. The female evangelist talked on faithfulness. It was the word I could not think of in the fruit of the Spirit list. Then the pastor got up and praised my work and used it as an example. He hadn't seen me in action, but my students had come to see him to tell of their new abilities. I was humbled, for the Lord has been in it. I again was asked to say something.

Day 20: Friday, December 9

Morris came and copied the punctuation mark, negative contractions, and review of long and short vowels. We put the motif of fire on the board: at Peter's denial, coldness and darkness; at Peter's reinstatement, care (an example from Jesus); and Pentecost, power of the Holy Spirit. Nathaniel had copied the equivalent chart of common fractions, decimals, and percents, but I noticed they were not perfectly aligned, so I helped him out. Finally, I gave him solutions to (1) ½ of 6 = N; (2) ½ N = 6; and (3) 6 N = ½. I wasn't sure why I needed to give that info, except to say there is more.

The women got all that plus synonyms of *said*, plus a bit more of how to write. While stragglers were finishing copying the work, four of us read of the woman caught in adultery (John 8:3–11), the one healed of bleeding, and the girl returned to life (Mark 5:21–43). Women's issues are important.

Morris and Nathaniel had brought over my big box in the morning, and the eight women were willing to take my direction to pack my things in it. They had learned that I have my ways of doing things. It took us forty minutes to pack and clean and all eight women to bring the box over to Marinda's house, including the one who brought the easels. Goodbye, ladies. See you at the final program!

Marinda served potato greens and chicken over rice. She baked coconut tarts and papaya pie. Yum! After dinner my student with perfect attendance, Rebecca, was asked that if she knew where money for school was coming from, would she stop using men for money? At fifteen, she had a one-and-a-half-year-old son. I will sponsor her and her son at $500 a year for fifteen to twenty years, if needed. Poverty kills. (A year plus later, her end of sixth grade report card showed passing grades; she excelled at Bible.)

At night the full moon rose. I was serenaded by the young men around the house and perhaps others. They left when I started singing to them, "I have the joy, joy, joy, joy, down in my heart." Marinda's voice is hoarse, worse than mine, but we belt out the old hymns. I just don't know all the words to them.

Saturday, December 10

It just took an hour to pack my big blue bag after breakfast. I'd given away lots, but supplies from the barrel had to go in. Marinda and I spent an hour or so in the library dusting and sorting books to be put in baskets for each class. All twelve grades, K-11, have "reading nooks" now.

After lunch of eggplant and chicken over rice, we just talked. "Sister" Martha wouldn't be there until three, at least. My clothes would dry.

Because of a flat tire and the need to put it in for repair, Martha, her little boy, and a new garbage can actually got to Marinda's at nearly five o'clock. All the household had returned from their pursuits, so I was able to say goodbye to them all. I especially told little Charles that I was leaving but would be back in nine weeks for a day. He had gotten his hand caught in a car door and was crying for awhile until Otally's magic touch soothed him. My easels were unhinged a bit; the little washers, nuts, and bolts were put in a plastic bag. At first, the boys flung them to the sand.

Along the way to the orphanage, the cab picked up the repaired spare tire. We went on paved roads, improved dirt roads, and finally the rutted lanes. Some beautiful homes had been gutted. Mostly I saw homes of bamboo with roofs of thatch or tin. The driver finally turned on his headlights, but he surely had to have had cat's eyes to be able to stay clear of uneven terrain. The full moon helped him.

The kids of the orphanage unloaded all the booty, and the cab disappeared. Then I sat in the classroom dining area while they sang me songs, including, "Lord, I Lift Your Name on High," one I knew! I was shown my bed, but then I asked to go to the bathroom. They took me around to another room; I waited while they filled the new garbage can with water from the river. The boys nimbly stepped on the slats leading to the entrance; the new cement wasn't quite dry yet. Not so steady on the boards myself, I used the new toilet in the room that would be mine the next day. Sister (not a nun but a title) Martha, who has sixty children in her orphanage, and I had fried plantain slices and hot tea. Yum!

With my plastic cup from home and bottled water from Marinda's care package, I flossed and brushed my teeth without a drain. Marinda had also provided a flashlight with fresh batteries and spares. When I got into her nice bed, Sister Martha put a mattress on the floor for herself and slept with a young charge. A nightlight kept everyone but me in peace. I used a t-shirt to cover my eyes. While I usually get up during the night, I used all my fleshly and divine powers not to. A good time was had by all.

Sunday, December 11

The room they've made just for me has a toilet and a new garbage can full of water at one end. Knowing I could get up easily at night made sleeping easier. I sat on a ledge to watch the activity of moving in but then was given a plastic chair. The painted ledge now has my undies, folded blouses, and school supplies.

As "guest," I have a table all to myself on the newly cemented veranda. It's in view of everyone who is coming and going. It's fun to see all the activity. The girls clean everything. At Marinda's I sat facing a wall and could see the bustle from the bedroom hallway into the pantry area. Marinda might sit with her back to the wall so she could survey her household, or she might be elsewhere. I then ate alone with my own thoughts, ignoring the others who were busy with their own activities. Here at the White Plains orphanage, my back is next to the wall. The chair was moved from inside to outside easily enough. A guest receives but has no control.

My first morning here was full of mystery and forbearance. My gear was in one place, and I managed to find clothes to put on. I at least could carry my small bag to my new room. The locksmith came and spent time hewing and reaming. His was a work of art. He entertained me while I waited for breakfast to be served.

There being time before church, I got out the easel sticks. Abbis and Marcus had loosened or unscrewed them so they could fit into the taxi space. I found the bag of pieces. One was easy to put together. I was glad I had it as a model. Of course I had an audience, so I started screwing to the tune of "I Have the Joy in My Heart." Unscrewing got the second verse, "love of Jesus." Soon both easels were complete. Many children had never seen an easel before. I'm not sure if everyone in Monrovia had, either.

Church was a ten- or fifteen-minute walk down the rutted dirt road. We passed the United Nations compound and saw the guards. All was well. St. Luke United Methodist Church in White Plains must have been really beautiful once. From the intact or merely broken colored windows, I could imagine what the missing pieces might be. The ceiling had been painted with a wine color on plywood. The choir loft in the upper back was still in an orderly shambles. The pews were old but serviceable. The altar and pulpit area had ornate, recently painted wine-and-blue carvings. Purple vestments were there for the Advent season.

A few of us went to church first. These young children kept me plied with open pages from the Methodist hymnal of 1968, given to them by churches in the United States. A few were ratty UMC hymnals of 1989. We sang them all. The choir sat in the section next to the altar and then came down to the front. I figured I should stop the "pre-singing." Soon the service started, with mostly the orphanage people leading and participating. The minister came wearing a collar. A deacon gave announcements. I was called on to tell what I was doing there; as the only white person, I had to have a reason for being there. I'm not sure whether he had been clued in ahead of time. He even indulged me and let me sing "There's a Voice in the Wilderness Crying" from the 1968 Book of Hymns since we'd read about John's coming.

The eleven o'clock service, which began at twelve ten with the securing of candles and then lighting them, was over. There was a lot of singing and liturgy. We walked back and waited for "lunch," which was served at three, with no meal later, though I was given hot tea.

At night the children performed for each other to the light of battery-operated lamps. By day I had read a primer on Liberia to them. A few preteen girls helped me unpack my box of supplies. It reminded me somewhat of *The Little Red Hen*, who had asked for help. The girls, however, wanted to help; I was entertainment, and they were curious. I also told a few Bible stories to the hangers-on. I was so tired during the orphanage evening service that I took up their suggestion and went to bed. A mosquito net had been set up.

Day 1: Monday, December 12

The first morning after a night in my new bedroom! My clothes were still in my big bag, but I managed to find something to wear for school. During the day, Sis Martha (Often honorary relationships are given

The Best to the Guest

to people; it is like saying *aunt* or *uncle* in the United States.) bought a pretty vanity shelf with hanger rod and a framed mirror. Both were nailed to the concrete wall with a rock. The debris from floor and ledge were cleaned. I now could spread out my clothes and unpack.

Two men came for learning, and two others came to watch and help. One student was young and apt; the other will take my ingenuity to new heights. He needs muscle training. He went from straight lines to large ovals. Progress! I'd asked for a circle. (George, a sixty-two-year-old student, had problems I could not alleviate. He was the sexton of St. Luke and fed by Martha. He never could draw a circle.)

One of the orphanage girls pretended to be a learner, but one of the attendants set us straight. There was too much smiling going on. One learner, Debora, came, and then four more. The letter R is not stressed in Liberia, though I think every name has one. They just can't spell their names, but they will. Debora came often but not enough to truly read. We fit in all the essential parts of Day 1: reading and writing *a, d, t, m, n*; Luke 10:25–28; *o, i*; numbers to 5; add and subtract to 5; odd and even; > <; and inch rulers to measure fingers. It was a good day.

Day 2: Tuesday, December 13

George came; I had a cup for him to hold. He was to make circles with his finger on the rim of the cup, top and bottom. James didn't come, but Tom did. He was apt to catch up since he actually was a teacher! Preachers and teachers came, too; I told them what I was about.

The women came. In Monrovia, most of the women knew the alphabet. These women did not. Nor could they rattle off the tenses of "to be." I must go slower. They were still working on mastering the first day's work while I added more: the "slippery consonants" (*h, r, l, s, w, y*), which change the vowel sounds whenever they feel like it. Unfortunately, I let them write from the big sheet. I hadn't allowed it in Monrovia; if they don't know letters, writing is premature.

I seemed to have settled in my room. Clothes were on the ledge, cosmetics on the vanity shelf. It was easy to transfer teaching props from my room to the teaching area: I'd move them out of my room onto a portico, and usually Samuel took them from portico through the porch of the girls' dormitory to the classroom. In the morning, children come over during their snack time to peek over the five-foot bamboo wall. In the afternoon, the chickens crow and cluck. Dogs and cats come anytime. My meals were served after each class (noon and five).

Day 3: Wednesday, December 14

Both James and Thomas returned, and three more men came. They seemed apt, but we had to go back to the basic *at, an, ad, am*, and the rest of the vowels. I guess the men and women need the same review for Thursday. When I reviewed subject pronouns, even George was repeating them. I wish I knew his history. I gave him a bottle cap to trace over, magnetic letters to pick up, and a special marker. While his dexterity is getting better, he still scribbles wildly.

The five women came and were still weak on short vowels. I gave them *b, g, p, ck*. We were ready to practice when two more women showed up. They could do the practice better than the first five. They needed printing skills, and I was ready to help them all.

Food was spicy here. I was served breakfast of potato, plantain, and one of pork, beef, or chicken (I'm not always sure). At lunch I got a tuna sandwich laden with onions on two pieces of white bread. I loved the wedge of cornbread. Dinner was often a vegetable or meat, usually chicken, over rice. I drank lots of bottled water and got hot tea for breakfast and late at night.

The children are fun. The young ones like me to sing from the hymn book. If my voice isn't shot, I do. The older ones clean, make my bed better, and try to be helpful. One girl took me to where others were bathing at the river. The lily pads were huge, but it wasn't where I'd like to swim or bathe.

Michael, a teacher of agronomy at the high school, will take me a week from Saturday to see some farming sites. I haven't been off the compound yet, except for church, so it sounds exciting.

Day 4: Thursday, December 15

Thomas was a ringer: he could read a scripture passage well, if not perfectly. We agreed he should not contribute to the phonics recitation, as that throws off the thinking of others. I threw out big words, and he would take those in. After dinner, I prepared an outline of 1Thessalonians for him to mull over. The other men need basic help and should get it.

Patience got to fourth grade ten years ago. She knows basic phonics. She will profit from the class, too. Just as I was trying to figure out how to present, as a review, the five short vowels, in came four more women! It was a teaching moment, albeit too much in too little space—sounds, letters, writing; fourteen consonants and five vowels. They came, got their supplies (composition book, pen, New Testament) and returned for only one more day, just as I was figuring out how I would manage.

Two adults expressed an interest in living in the United States. I could help them, but I don't want to be responsible for them. One sells candy. Another teaches and works at the orphanage. The candy man, Samuel, is handy with tools.

At dinner a dog and a cat faced me longingly. Another dog was nearby. The cat inched closer. When it finally made a leap to the top of the table, I batted it away. They resumed their adoration, which stopped when the food was carted away. They are fed elsewhere.

Day 5: Friday, December 16

Four more men came. They could write their names and could profit from a review of short *a* and long *a*. Only Adolphus and Thomas came from before. I helped Adolphus with borrowing. The new ones could do that but did not know polygons. We reviewed perimeter.

In the afternoon, Zenan returned, and two new students who looked like orphan kids. One was, but the other had been in kindergarten and first grade. I could help them add. All students from the day before were missing—too much Christmas prep and sick children. There is no continuity, but disillusionment.

I watched the boys play soccer and volleyball. When the official volleyball stopped, I played a bit. It felt good after so little exercise; I felt weak. I've taught some of the girls "The Twelve Days of Christmas." They needed copies, and I wrote them out by flashlight. Then I told more Bible stories. Hopefully they could hear and understand me better than I could them.

Saturday, December 17

All of us seemed to wake up a little later today. It was real daylight when I saw my hand. No one was attending the fires for breakfast. How strange! Soon, though, the camp awoke.

My breakfast was a sliced boiled egg, Navy bean, potato, and mayo combo. It was good. For lunch I got more beans, with crackers and papaya. I seem also to get freshly squeezed orange juice. Dinner was yam and chicken leg over rice. At evening snack, I was served a wedge of cassava cake, or something.

Early in the day, I got out my short vowel cards and taught the kids how to play Go Fish. Supposedly they were to ask for what rhymed, but they only named the last two letters. It was a running card game for five players for two or three hours. Some of the older boys played with me. They could hear, so they spoke for me. I taught them to listen for what the others were asking, and if we had it, to ask for it at our turn. All were quick to learn it. I taught a girl to play Concentration, too.

The kids were shooed away at lunchtime, but the game resumed in their play area, where I teach. After I ate dinner, somehow it migrated back to my table in the form of Concentration. I called a halt when it was so dark I couldn't see the words on the cards, even though the kids could. There was light enough for the volleyball and soccer at the school yard. I watched and kicked the soccer ball a bit. It was a new experience. All that playtime ended when curfew began at 6:30, though there was still light and space to do exercises. The kids followed my lead. I'd been sitting all day: reading an old, just-opened *Reader's Digest* (I have one more in English and three in Spanish to open and read). My plastic chair was comfortable for relaxing.

A devotional period took place in the darkness except for a few lanterns spread around. I can't understand the songs and prayer chants, but I can move and pray in Christ's name.

During the night, returning from a potty break, I went too far and sat down on the floor instead of my bed. I got up with no ill effects (thank you, God), glad for the earlier limbering up.

Sunday, December 18

Breakfast was applesauce cake with hot tea. I was served my lunch before going to church since my server would be going elsewhere and return late: chicken with spicy noodles and onions over rice. Before leaving for church, some of us were suffering from not having much to do. I was happy to entertain by singing "Deep and Wide," "Jesus Loves the Little Children," and "I Have the Joy …" The younger kids loved it. When the older ones started on the rock music, we realized it was time to go.

The advance party got to St. Luke's and started our singing ritual from the hymn books. At eleven the youth choir took over, but then the leader left. We found out the minister couldn't come. I went back to ask if we could have a leader of service. They could if I would preach. Okay, I'd think of something. The service proceeded. I got to sing most of the hymns. The kids kept me supplied with the right page.

Since they read Matthew 1:17–23, we had Joseph's take on the birth of Jesus: just in the nick of time. It was the fourth Sunday of Advent, when we are looking for the second coming of Jesus. I reverted to the study of 1 and 2 Thessalonians I'd been reading for five weeks in Liberia. The Thessalonians had thought Jesus was coming real soon and had stopped working. Paul praised and admonished through exhortation. I praised the hard work of the children at the orphanage and also the restoration work going on at the church. While we wait for celebrating the first and second coming, we can hold Jesus Christ in our hearts. I sang and led "I Have the Joy in My Heart" and prayed. The parishioners clapped (I found out they did that with the regular minister, too); we had been edified.

Back home, the kids asked for the cards. I played one game but let them continue without me. I needed to work on lesson plans, for I was hopelessly behind. Professor Peter had come around after my breakfast asking my take on Romans 5:4—problems lead to character to endurance and hope. That reminded me of my lesson plan situation. I must simply do the lesson for the quorum that comes. This Christmas season wasn't helping consistency of attendance. I could not have done this ten years ago. I had become much more flexible and could laugh at roosters and other disturbances.

The teen girls invited me to play kickball in the soccer field. Then we played volleyball. I served, and my side eventually won the game. It was dumb luck, but I do know how to serve. Later we went to a field past the church. We entered the shell of a huge home of people who attended St. Luke UMC. A young lady who knew how to pitch changed into shorts. I was in seventh heaven, getting to walk a long way and to see different sights, but the sun even at four thirty was not good for me. I watched from under a "triple" tree: three trees together. A palm tree with pompom shoots at the top of the triple made for an interesting study. I wished I had my camera; next time I will. Another tree was well filled out, but only at its edges to take in the sunlight.

I got home after my usual dinnertime at five. Other girls returned even later. The staff fed them first. I got my meal during the snack at eight o'clock: two large fritters with hot tea. I was happy to get them and said they looked good. They tasted good, too. Endurance!

Day 6: Monday, December 19

I washed my clothes and towels. Yes, the girls assigned to me would do it better, but my laundry was already up and drying. My patio space was being cleaned as I wrote in my journal. Now I was ready for devotions, having washed clothes and self, dressed, and hung out laundry (a daily routine).

It was the week before Christmas. The adults were trying to earn a dime to give gifts to their families. Women prepared the homes.

Adolphus and two new men showed up for class. They did short and long *i* and *e*, the rest of the consonants, and prepositions. They were at the same math place: subtraction with borrowing. I couldn't get them to see the concept.

Only Debora showed up for the women's class. She'd missed Thursday and Friday, so I gave her quite a review. She could add without carrying but needed help with carrying. I had given out my quota of pens, composition books, and New Testaments. I would have to give any newcomers only paper and pencils; sharing a Bible isn't the same.

After dinner (yams and something else over rice), I went to the road to see what I could see. A few men were kicking a soccer ball; others were at the volleyball net. One fellow was putting palm branches in bags while stuffing charcoal in the spaces. The bags were carted off on the heads of younger boys, who had a cloth ring to protect them. Some men were standing around looking at another's new toy that made noise. A two- or three-year-old girl (who I found out was really a boy named Rufie) latched herself onto me and got me to kick a dilapidated soccer ball with her. It was my speed, and I got pretty good—kind of—for that league. After playtime outside the compound was over, I led some exercises and danced La Raspa inside to some girls who watched and imitated my every move.

The Monday night devotions had a hardcore preacher giving a saving message. Many came to the altar for saving/rededication. This orphanage was run by Christian Aid Ministries, a very conservative organization. I have enjoyed telling the youngsters some Bible stories at their request, even though they have Bible studies in school.

Day 7: Tuesday, December 20

Today my mother, Mary Wegner, turned ninety-six in Crozet, Virginia.

Since I had given out all my supplies, I gave a young man paper and pencil. He didn't stick around for the conclusion of the day. We were using my New Testament; I could read upside down. I helped George with addition: I wrote the numbers, and he did the thinking. His mind is good, but his hand movements, speech, and eyesight are faulty. I can't teach it away.

Three women from the first day of class came. We had a good time with prepositional phrases from a scripture passage.

I saw nail clippers on a key chain and expressed a desire to use them. Gormai was amenable. Thus, while they copied, I got my bucket to soak my hands and feet and clipped five and a half weeks' worth of nails. The foot cuticles were clean, and I felt so feminine. The good cooking here made my hands look beautiful.

These women were on the cusp of a reading breakthrough; they swore they would be there the next day, when I was hoping to go to Monrovia to see Marinda's Christmas program.

For dinner I had spiced shrimp (crawdads) over rice. Afterward, I saw the girls practicing their volleyball skills. Later, I sat beside a fifteen-year-old girl who was feeding one of the two babies in the compound. The other baby had been fed. Bench seats and backs were made of bamboo, as were the tall fence posts surrounding the compound. Finally, I got to my seat by my door, danced to the music, had my tea, and told the stories of Jesus's early ministry. We were shooed to bed; I don't argue with the boss!

Day 8: Wednesday, December 21

George came to class today. I had him draw a dog; it was a few scribbles. He had a big brown dog that liked to run fast. We talked about adjectives and adverbs. He knows a lot, but he can't translate it to his hands.

I then showed him and lots of children during the day some autumn pictures of red, orange, and yellow trees and told how leaves fall. Trees are bare of leaf in winter, and it snows. I at least had a picture of penguins in the snow of Antarctica. I figured the calendars I brought would have snow in them, but they didn't. In spring the nodes on branches become buds and then burst into leaves. In Liberia there are two seasons: dry and rainy. Leaves stay green on the trees all year round; however, some fall every day.

No women showed. I could have gone to the Christmas program in Monrovia, but I didn't want to pay the $50 cab fare and ride for one to two hours each way.

The electrician came to the compound and put in fluorescent bulbs, light switches, and electric sockets at strategic points. I got one of each. The generator worked at three o'clock for the man but not when I could use it at night. He made a mess on my blouses, which I'd offered to move, but he'd insisted it wasn't necessary. I dusted them off outside. My cleaner came in and swept. I washed the ledge of dust. Things got back to normal. The electrician and I each apologized. I said I was upset about another matter and took it out on him.

Dinner was served at four o'clock, not my usual five. I put my teaching supplies away and ate shrimp and yams over rice. Delicious! I went walking to the right and found a lake behind me. The neighbors had access to it; my student Zenan took me to it. Access was a steep incline, which I didn't feel like tackling. Two men did, though, easily. Later, some girls and boys were playing jump rope with electrician's wires. They were good at it. Returning, I led the smaller ones in exercises; they wanted La Raspa, too. I don't like to do it in flip-flops, but they think nothing of it. My feet are no longer tough.

Day 9: Thursday, December 22

I wasn't expecting many, if any, students to come. George did, and I showed him the map of the United States I made in front of him. I only got to forty-six states and finally added Minnesota. Thomas showed up and made me a map of Liberia and its counties. Monrovia and White Plains are both in Monserrado County. White Plains is on the way from Ganta to the Monrovian airport. I would need that info in five weeks. Perhaps Barry could return me from his preacher conference.

Polly Riddle

Adolphus and Prince showed up after George. It was adverb and adjective day. Adolphus could almost read my opposites (big-little) list. Prince could already. Debora showed up for the women. With effort she did read the list. It is designed for using lots of context clues. It was again breakthrough time. I was gratified. She was beginning to follow the scripture passage if I went slowly and broke it up.

After dinner—slices of wiener with spices and yam over rice—I went to the rise in the road and saw a volleyball game with a good ball and youngsters with a dilapidated soccer ball. Michael showed up to confirm our nine o'clock date on Saturday; he'll show me around his farm.

Day 10: Friday, December 23

Adolphus and George showed up. We did soft *g* and *c*, *r*-controlled words, reviewed cards from previous lessons, and read about the magi. Debora did the same in the afternoon. She also helped me pack my box of supplies I needed in Ganta, where Barry would lead a preacher's conference. Most of the New Testaments were in a box for composition books. There was definitely less to cart around. I would be leaving for Ganta right after Christmas with Mark, who was coming shortly from the United States. Both Barry and Mark were part of Compassion Corps, who planned my stay in Liberia.

The neighbor down the road from the orphanage compound was pregnant. Both she and the baby died today. She was Prince's aunt. Many have interrupted Christmas prep to see the bereft family. Sister Martha and I went up to see them, but the family had gone.

Christmas Eve: Saturday, December 24

The children have been practicing a singing Christmas program for church on Sunday. A few individuals have wished me Merry Christmas, but there is not a single shred of decoration in the compound.

As promised, Michael, teacher of agriculture and literature at the school across the street, took me through the brush past the school. The teachers of Jesus Christ Children's International High School hope to clear the land and grow cassava, a lucrative cash crop. I was shown how it was grown, from planting and growth of leaves to harvesting at eight months or so. They use a hand machete and hoe but dream of seeds and machines. They hope to raise not only their own food but also enough to earn money for a library and clinic, costing $200,000. I gave him $5, two old *Reader's Digests*, and a prayer. I took pictures and will talk about the dream when I get home. Marinda has first priority, however.

I also was taken down to the St. Paul River, where I got my picture taken. (I have pictures of me in or near water from all over the world.) Evidently, Michael had never been down that steep incline, but when he saw that I did it, he could not refuse! I'm more than twenty years his senior. Across the river was where President Sirleaf was born and grew up. I took a picture of youngsters at the plantain trees. Both plantain and cassava are good for protein. In the compound itself, I photographed the potato and collard greens growing. Then I washed out my sneakers, socks, and pedal pushers. The Liberian sun would dry them.

Mark was coming. He represented Compassion Corps, which provided funds and know-how. The people swept, cleaned, put up welcome posters, and arranged a palm branch arch. A table was prepared for his dinner. He didn't come and didn't tell Sister Martha, who had made the laborious trip to the airport for him. Ganta knew, but no one had informed Martha. Nor did Ganta want Polly. I spent a night full of stomach gas. (I found out later the Ganta ministry would be in the hinterland, evangelizing.)

Christmas Day: Sunday, December 25

I woke and remembered and listed the fruit of the Spirit. I thanked the Lord for Jesus, who came in humble circumstances. I was thankful for the sun, the fun I had with the little ones, the people who cooked and cleaned and guided, the ones who cared for the babies. The gas in my body stopped. I washed my hair, body, and clothes (all usual for a Sunday). When I hung my clothes out, all of the orphanage had assembled in the meeting space, but I hadn't been invited and went back inside my room. Perhaps I hadn't heard the invitation, but I didn't want to horn in on their intimacy. I had my own devotions to read and meditate on. Today was Daniel 6; he was faithful.

The eleven o'clock service started at twelve ten, when the candles were lit. We sang lots of Christmas carols with limited involvement of kids. They served rice and fufu afterward. I helped an elderly lady get something to drink. Back at the compound, I ate popcorn with Sis Martha and Michael.

Later in the afternoon Martha, Michael, and I set off for the house where the pregnant one had died. The husband, grandmother, and children were there. After a suitable time of silence and words, I offered a prayer of presence from the Prince of Peace and God of All Comfort.

Hair styling was the order of the day at the orphanage, just as it was in Monrovia: lots of stylists, lots of extra hair, lots of heads to work on. I enjoyed it all. One girl combed my bouffant hair straight. They all remarked how beautiful I was and smiled. I kept my opinion secret.

The orphanage program was at seven. The first number was my leading the smaller children in "The Twelve Days of Christmas." I'd never heard them sing so lustily. Bible reading and a pantomime about the birth of Jesus ensued. I was close to the action, but in the semi-darkness I still could not understand the spoken word.

I was given the opportunity to preach and told about the catechism of the twelve days of Christmas: 1 God, 2 testaments, 3 trinity or patriarchs, 4 gospel writers, 5 books of the law, 6 days of creation, 7 abominations (Proverbs 6 or deadly sins someplace), 8 people saved in Noah's ark, 9 Fruit of the Spirit, 10 commandments, 11 disciples in heaven, and 12 disciples or tribes of Israel. If they couldn't remember all that, they could at least be thankful for something. Gratitude had helped me get rid of my sour stomach.

Sister Martha brought out the dolls I'd brought from the friend of Judie, the organist at St. Andrew's. They'd been used as ballast for the big, heavy box. First the younger children and then the older ones who wanted them received a doll. It seemed all who wanted, got. It was a Spirit-filled time of awe. After the program, I was served tea. Michael cut up a lumpy lime. Someone squeezed it into my cup. How tart and delicious! He and another man had some tea with lime, also.

Second Day of Christmas: Monday, December 26

Sunday is not a day to play, so this was the day to celebrate Christmas. I really saw no difference, except there was no church. On Sunday the children were given pretty clothes. Today they got play clothes. Prince, whose aunt had just died, came over to get a lesson from the gospel of John on foot washing. After lunch he and another boy, Joe, asked me how Christmas was celebrated in the United States. I told them about parties, cookies, decorations, creches, and trees.

Dinner was special. They served water in new purple cups. While rice was served in their usual bowls, which had been washed thoroughly, extra meat was heaped on it. Usually there is just a dollop of meat. I got rice with what I think were pieces of chicken. I thought at first it was beef ribs. It had collard greens cooked in palm oil all around it.

After dinner Joe took me for a walk. Lots of others went too, but Joe was my "date." Girls his age, fourteen or fifteen years old, swarmed around him, but he gently spurned them. We went into the UN compound. All of us were invited into a tent to watch television, but I wanted none of that. Joe got the boss to show us the water filtration plant they run for Liberia, especially Monrovia. Water from the river is purified with sulfate and chlorine. Since I was a VIP of sorts, they gave the two of us a complete tour. After the UN gambit, we continued past the church to the big house, got invited to hear some music, stayed for a tune or two, and then left. I could have walked to the field by turning right, but I didn't feel like it. Going straight was off-limits. On the way home, I saw the "daddy fellow" I'd met earlier with his daughter of seven months; I met his wife and mother, also.

At play, one of the girls gashed her foot. Martha washed it somewhat and sterilized it. I gave some Neosporin, two Band-Aids, and an Ace bandage to hold them on. Then I played soccer, kind of, with the baby that could walk.

At the devotional period, I was asked to speak again. I told of my mother, now ninety-six, who had lived in an orphanage from ages six to eighteen, got her degree, married a chemist, and had two children.

Others in that orphanage had become judges and other persons of influence. This was to remind them they would not always be children in an orphanage. Then I compared Jesus and his importance, who was willing to be a servant and wash the disciples' feet. We must remember servanthood with greatness.

Third Day of Christmas: Tuesday, December 27

Spring cleaning, Liberia style! Lots of boxes of canned chicken from Christian Aid, inspected by the USDA, were brought out of storage. Sacks of flour and rice were stacked. Joe, Prince, and other young men flexed their muscles to help lift them. A few games, paddle balls, and yo-yos were found. Bags of clothes were processed and given out. I sat at my table trying, at points, to study the gospel of Mark, and other times showing calendars and pictures of fall was in order. I got out the digraph/consonant cluster domino game and taught it to a few kids. We played three rounds. Then it was time to walk around.

What I really wanted to do was to irrigate my ears and did. One girl got me hot water, and another one brought me cups of cold water to make it just-right warm. Another was willing to drink the excess water. (Waste not, want not.) One put drops in my ears. If I'm doing it by myself, I normally get more bang from the dropper, but I had enough for this day (and no more) and the one application in Monrovia the previous month. I did not have a mirror to help me. Some wax filtered out: very small flakes. Some water dripped on my pants; one girl tried to make it better and spilled the whole thing. I'd tried to stop her, but it was too late. Rather than get angry, a former trait of mine, I laughed, changed, and put the pants to dry in the nice Liberian sun.

Sister Martha mixed bread dough. We had homemade rolls at snack/devotional time. My roll may have had cheese in it. It's hard for me to check it out in the darkness. It was good, as was the hot tea. Before the snack, Prince and Joe asked me what was happening in Philadelphia. I told them about preparing for the Mummers parade on New Year's Day. Sports—basketball, football, ice hockey—were in full gear in the city.

My church was closed for the week so that families could be together. I told them of my many activities at my senior center: swimming, square dancing, billiards, ping pong, wheelchair attendant at chapel, and cards.

After dinner I wandered over to the classrooms where Mark was to be housed and saw a woman and children. While I thought they were part of the orphanage, she told me her group was on a retreat with her youth from Monrovia. She invited me to speak the next day; she also said that cleaning was traditional after Christmas in order to have a clean house for the new year. In the "small world" category, she said she worked with John at Scripture Union.

Fourth Day of Christmas: Wednesday, December 28

Hump day! I've spent half my allotted time in Liberia and look forward to the second half. I inscribed a New Testament for Joe, whose fifteenth birthday is today: "Manhood is many things at many ages; live in integrity and gratitude. Galatians 5:22–23 helps, too." He came by early, and I happily gave him my offering. Then in a letter he asked for money, the same amount that I had given Prince after his aunt had died. My joy faded at feeling used. I told him I didn't have it. Prince needed money after his aunt died, but Joe was getting all his needs met at the orphanage. Food for thought!

I was given a T-shirt to wear for my talk about my calls to preach, to come to Liberia, and on being a bridge to so many people. The camp is sponsored by New and Living Way Ministries for a Pentecostal church. Its theme was Romans 8:1: with Jesus we don't have to live in sin. I'd had on a blouse from Honduras, but I changed into the T-shirt. I spoke for half an hour, gave the leader a New Testament, and slipped a note for them to give to John to give to Marinda. I would be returning to them two weeks early and wanted to share my thoughts of how to use the time.

I was able to study and make notes on Mark. That's a feat, for many come to stay to kibbitz or just *be*. I tried to be open to need and opportunity. After lunch I got out the cluster /digraph domino game.

There is little phonemic awareness here. Later they threw the soccer ball for me to kick; I'm improving.

Prince came by for a lesson in his New Testament, but we had to walk first to give me air in my lungs. We read the call of Nathaniel in John 1 and then from John 21, where Peter went fishing with his friends. Prince helped me realize how low a fund of concepts a person can live on.

After dinner—beans and chicken over rice—I went to see the action at the volleyball and soccer venues. It was fun to see it all. Then I came back in for a Bible study; at least I could understand clapping. The younger girls joined me later and sang with me; they were in full voice and excited. I loved it. Prince and Joe just didn't have a chance for my attention.

Fifth Day of Christmas: Thursday, December 29

Lots of quilts were aired on the bamboo clothes lines. The usual clothes dried on the rest of the bamboo, on the tin roofs of the buildings, and under the eaves where the evening dew would not get to them.

In the morning, I studied more of Mark. Then I got out the rhyming cards and had whatever kids were there to identify the pictures: game, frame, flame, name. We played the digraph/cluster domino game. I also got the rest of the pictures out. The younger children have very little phonemic awareness, even at second grade. Slides, frames, clowns, swings, and other items we take for granted are not around.

In return, I got to kick the soccer ball and play volleyball. They love to mimic my exercises, sing, and dance La Raspa. At night we even did the Hokey Poky and other American songs. Near dinner, the group from Monrovia came over to say goodbye.

After dinner—kidney beans and something masquerading as ground beef, which could be greens of sorts, over rice—I went over to watch the highly rated soccer match, the UMs versus somebody else. While I had to leave because I was getting red, I watched each team score. The orphanage youth choir practiced in the dim light; they certainly can sing.

Sixth Day of Christmas: Friday, December 30

The older children came to see about my phonics cards. They'd been encouraged by Sis Martha. In the afternoon, I got the tiles out and allowed them to test their skills for real. They didn't know: straw, garden hose, mask, and so many others. The items just aren't experienced here. Prince came and wanted to read the letter to the Hebrews; I'm glad I'd studied it. We read the first chapter. We never got to a second chapter.

As I was ensconced with children watching and doing around the table, one of them brought my dry towel from the sun. While my thoughts centered about not needing this gift, I said, "Thank you" and put it on my chair. I often use "checking my clothes" as an excuse to walk someplace. I didn't get my usual dose of play. As it is, I'm losing muscle strength.

We were to have an all-night prayer time in the meeting area. I got to reading Isaiah, chapters 40–66, for my prayer basis. Suddenly at nine o'clock, it was all over. I finished the passage in my room. Perhaps I misunderstood.

Seventh Day of Christmas: Saturday, December 31

I washed self and clothes, as usual, and read my Bible. Breakfast was served while I read the Spanish commentary on 1 Timothy 2:15–18. The word *head* can mean *source*. Adam's rib was the source of Eve, from whence she came. The Trinity has a mutuality, not a pecking order. In Ephesians Paul was trying to deter, or "head off," the beginning of the Gnosticism heresy, as well as asceticism, which denied one's having children. Often these religions put Eve first in appearance. Paul was about order and decorum in dress, worship, and life in general.

The children came around early and played my domino game. Michael had come around, and I talked about life on the Pacific Coast, the Mississippi from Chicago to New Orleans, and the Everglades. We got to New York, Maryland, and Washington, DC. He recognizes I'm also knowledgeable about the environment.

After lunch I got out my rhyming cards and let one child put the rhyming tiles on five cards. She had quite the audience and lots of help. I gave another child five more cards and their tiles. They all enjoyed that one, too. When I put them away and returned, the very young little boys were there. I sent them away, getting help for it. For a half hour, I read my Spanish *Reader's Digest,* and for another half hour I studied Mark. There is nothing like having time alone to regroup.

When I went "exploring," the older girls invited me for a "walk." They said something else, but my hearing was bad and could only understand *walk*. I changed into socks and sneakers and was led to the right, past the known house where Prince lives. They told me the United Methodists were meeting in the high-back chairs on the left, but we weren't going there; I'd have fit very nicely in their retreat. Instead, we went right, down an incline that showed my moxie. I was stepping on bamboo leaves and branches and almost falling as I hurled my body down; my shoes had very little tread. The boys were cutting bamboo for the girls to take back as firewood. I stayed clear of the cutting area and watched. Such agility! I hoisted a tube of bamboo and brought it up the incline; while gravity had taken over on the way down, I worked hard at finding purchase and traction going up. At the signal to return to camp, I picked up the log and alternated shoulders for its transport. The girls had picked vines along the way and used them to tie three times the weight of my bundle and carried their burden on their heads. Boys cut; girls transported. (On other days boys transported long bamboo poles.) My one log was a photo-op back at the compound.

At that point, I could play dominoes again. After three games, my limit, I put it away and got out the four magnetic cards with their respective digraph, blends, long vowels, and short vowels, beginning and final. Even the older ones had to ask what things are. Americans might need to know about bamboo. I thought it grew only in China for the pandas.

After dinner—spicy stew with potatoes, carrots, and beef over rice—I went to the soccer match across the road. The United Methodists won the championship. I happened to talk to Harrison, an organizer for the United Methodist team. He took my e-mail address, but I told him "no promises" for anything.

Coming back, I was encouraged to pick up the six- or seven-month-old, who hated me. So I did. Such a wail! Others knew of her antipathy, and one came to comfort her while I held her. She calmed down, and I was able to take her around and talk to her. I was glad to set her down well with her caretaker. Then I took the opportunity to dance and exercise.

I had my snack of hot tea and peanut butter sandwich and then prepared to go to St. Luke UMC for the watch night service. We left at nine or so. Many of the youngsters fell asleep in the pews immediately. Some adults were also asleep before the service. I was wired. The ten o'clock service began at ten twenty. The preacher and his helper had put spotlights at side front, where the pulpit was, and the other side back where the scaffolding was. Both were photo-ops, but I wasn't quick enough. I loved seeing the agility of the pastor. Some ceiling fans had been added since last Sunday, but they were not on.

There's no organ or piano, so the pastor does his best at pitching the hymns. When he lets the youth choir sing, they use the native shakers. They need to bring some wood for bongos; at the compound they use chairs. Using the pews would be okay with me, but it might seem disrespectful. I don't understand what the pastor says. He looks at his notes and his shoes when he speaks. When he sings the Gloria and Praise after some readings, he immediately turns toward the altar. The Lord's Prayer is sung in a chant automatically. I'm getting better at following it all. The children try to help me find the right hymn page. Sometimes I have just gone up and looked at his page number. We sing the same hymns each week, even at this watch night service.

New Year's Day and the Eighth Day of Christmas: January 1, 2012

The preacher announced the beginning of the new year. My watch still had two minutes to go, but we wished everyone happy New Year with hugs and handshakes. Then there was spontaneous dancing: I let loose with my jig, La Raspa, cha-cha, and "Joy" song. The boys formed a line and snaked around the pews. Women served rolls and hot chocolate or something. I gave my roll to a girl, who passed it around for several to take. The choir re-sang their praise song, and we clapped and swayed. I sang "O for a Thousand Tongues to Sing" and was among the first group to leave at one a.m.

It was chilly going home, but the stars were out in their glory. I went to bed, but during the night I had to get up and put my skirts onto my bed for warmth. Dawn came, and I awoke to start the New Year's Day with washing and breakfast of a sloppy Joe. Writing in my diary and devotions came afterward.

St. Luke UMC was not meeting for the regular Sunday service, so we went to the Zion Church near the tree I wanted to photograph. The church had cute doodads hanging from the ceiling and pulpit. I was accorded a plastic chair in the aisle. Others fit into pew/school desk affairs. Sister Martha and others got chairs in the other aisle. The pastor was just finishing Sunday School when we came in. He was in a yellow shirt, which reminded me of the Caribbean dress shirts I've seen. The man dressed in a suit was the service leader, who I had originally thought was the pastor. We praised God with bongos, shakers, and dancing for over an hour. That also included a dance up to the offering box. The dais was a raised platform covered with Liberian linoleum two thirds of the way. The minister preached from the altar area and the front of it, too, on Daniel 10:10. Daniel's prayer was answered, but there was such interference that the angel had to wait for reinforcements. We need help, too, from our buddies who have differing abilities. The pastor had been to my class and prayed for me from the pulpit.

Some children went with me to photograph the three-part tree. Naturally, they got into the picture, too, including Joe and Prince. On the way home, a girl made a switch from a reed along the road. I told her not to hit anyone with it, and she tossed it to the ground. I have seen too much play-hitting in the last few days. They have started jabbing one another, too.

I'm fighting a possible sore throat and was gratified for the orange served me at lunch. Afterward I got out the four magnetic phonics boards. How glad I was when the younger kids left and the older, more knowledgeable ones came. My throat needed a rest.

Lights powered by the generator came on, to everyone's joy! The kids gathered where the TV was and waited for a video to be played. Getting the video going was a learning opportunity for the older boys, and they finally succeeded. I was interested in its being played but not in watching. I had my snack, read a bit with my light, and then went to bed. With hearing aids removed and a T-shirt over my head and eyes, I could deal with sound and light from the next room.

Ninth Day of Christmas, Day 11 of Teaching: Monday, January 2

The sweeping brigade to clean the classroom was late and my breakfast a bit early. The latter was great, but I hate to eat in the midst of dust. They were preparing my classroom, so I was able to get my teaching boards only as far as my table. Even so, the sweepers arranged only eight chairs and desks rather than all sixteen. A student and I remedied that, since I did not want a hodgepodge arrangement.

Michael was a student in the twelfth grade at the school but not an orphan. He wanted to see the phonics presentation, so I accommodated him. He got all short and long vowel sheets and both pronoun sheets, which included the verb "to be." By that time, another reader had come, and we enjoyed reading Acts 27:27–44, Paul and the shipwreck. I'd learned to pre-tell the story, write down the setting and characters, and draw pictures of the ship. We talked about plot at the end. In math I briefly displayed the sheets showing place value of numbers and how to read them. Fun!

My lunch at noon was the same as the children's. They took over the classroom, which is also their main meeting room. I waited until ten of two, grabbed my wash rag, and wiped off the desks. Usually someone else had that chore. I let a girl rinse out the rag and return it to me. It dried on a railing of the classroom wall.

Kamah, a new woman, came. She'd been to third grade. I still reviewed long and short vowels. Gormai came and got with the review.

While I don't know what she has learned, I know the review was helpful. While Kamah copied lots of sheets, Gormai and I looked at my picture book. I'd saved my work-up of the shipwreck and showed the maps of where the Adriatic Sea is, as I did with the men. Kamah could do subtraction; Gormai was shaky at addition.

I was served promptly at five and then told the devotions were also at five. Usually they are after sundown at six thirty or seven. As the speaker for the event, I told them of the hitting and jabbing I'd seen recently, using parts of Matthew 5 and 7:12 as my text. You don't do it to yourself; don't do it to others. They got the message. It took a lot out of me to say it; was fighting that sore throat emotionally and physically and had to think affirming thoughts: *God is good all the time; all the time, God is good*. It worked for me.

Tenth Day of Christmas, Day 12 of Teaching: Tuesday, January 3

Two readers came for the men's class, including Gormai's husband, who had also come on Monday. When Prince arrived, I had someone to teach. We talked about consonant clusters, syllable making, and *ou, ow*. I showed them my *house* chart. Prince is ready for multiplication, having learned to borrow.

No women showed. The children wanted my phonics cards, so I got them out. It was a good afternoon. After dinner—beans and chicken over rice—we danced and had devotions. Was my purpose here for the kids and not adults?

Eleventh Day of Christmas, Day 13 of Teaching: Wednesday, January 4

Samuel, the candy seller, came in this morning, and I taught the lesson. When he went to his kiosk, I sat with George and wrote down for him words for *port, -mit, act, -ceive,* and *-lieve*. I had started prefixes and suffixes. We also reviewed a second-grader's Liberian math book, which dealt with everything I want to teach my adult students. I'm on track!

In the afternoon I told the children they could play with the cards if no one showed up. I went over my material, and Gormai showed up. I distributed the cards anyway and told the children not to bug me. I happily went over the *y to i and add -es, -er, or -est, doubling when needed*. I showed the alphabet with capitals and lower case letters; when *o* is a short *u* sound; *aw, au*; and *al, -all, -alm, -alk* words. We read John 8:1–12, the woman caught in adultery. For math I showed Gormai how to count and figure with her fingers and used the flash cards. She got it! Another breakthrough!

Dinner was waiting for me—some kind of fish over somewhat-flavored rice. The cats meowed; one got up on a chair, but I batted it away. I don't feel guilty eating it all, but I wish the cats could have some, too. I went out to the road to watch the pick-up soccer and volleyball games, but the children needed song and dance TLC worse. I got my exercise, too. It was fun to play.

We had devotions at the youth meeting where I teach. I sat at my table, stood, and clapped on cue, but understood nothing since my poor hearing interfered.

Twelfth Day of Christmas, Day 14 of Class: Thursday, January 5

When no men students came but Samuel, who came to rest in a comfortable chair, I went through my paces of prefix/suffix, with *port* and *-script/scribe* as examples. I even read the coming of the Magi from Matthew 2:1–12.

Then Michael, an overseer of Christian Aid Ministries, came on his motorcycle. He was there to check on things. When he returned to see what I was about, I showed him my teaching sheets and boards. Since he was a "student," I gave him a New Testament, composition book, and pen. My conscience would not allow me to withhold the bounty. I'd been shown earlier how meagerly the CAM supported the orphanage.

He, too, encouraged me to write the book of my teaching plans, even though it changes every time it is taught.

Later, when I started to cough, I drank more water. After lunch, I rigged up a big pillow and napped for a bit.

Four women came for afternoon classes, but I was ready for them. It was fun showing and explaining. For math, three students copied the addition/subtraction table chart. Then we reviewed working on our fingers. Gormai's ability stayed stable, showing the finger placement. Using hands to add became easy. The other woman, Kamah, got a dose of multiplication and division with the 2s facts.

My coughing from a draining head was worse, so I decided to stay quiet—no singing or dancing. I did help Prince, the nephew of the pregnant aunt who died. I helped him read scripture. At night I slept propped up.

Respect and Rest Day: Friday, January 6

I was feeling poorly, with sore throat and cough. I was glad we'd canceled classes out of respect for Prince's aunt. Her wake would be that night, and the women would be needed for cooking and whatever.

A printer was brought in to be set up. It printed a map I'd made of Palestine. Then I found out I had given that printer to Compassion Corps out of Ira's largesse. He had died two and a half years before. His toys continued to be used for the glory of God. Tears came as I told of it to Sis Martha.

By eating breakfast on my "verandah," I got to see the hustle and bustle of children and adults as they scurried to get ready for the day. The shower, whatever it was, and privy were all at the back. The bedrooms were in front, so I saw a lot of females passing back and forth with towels as drapes and other scanty, makeshift clothing. They emerged as school children dressed in red or white blouses and green skirts or jumpers or as ladies fully dressed for work. The five dogs lazed in the sun on the dirt, which I normally got to see swept, too. The two cats found a sunny place to lick their fur. I petted one kitty and let her curl up on the chair

I was using as a footstool; the chair became very dusty. Tired, I took two hours to read my Spanish commentary from 1 Timothy 4:1–16.

In the afternoon, I was trying to read my *Reader's Digest* but kept nodding off. One of the teens urged me to go to bed, so I did for two or three hours. That helped my system. I was able to sing and dance with the little ones again. They crave my TLC.

After dinner—spaghetti and chicken over rice—four of us women went down the lane to the wake. The body of the woman was decked out in an elaborate hat and dress and placed in a beautifully polished wood coffin lined with pink ruffled satin. Music blared from a speaker. A few danced to it. Others stood around or sat on makeshift seats of bamboo under a canopy constructed of bamboo and plastic sheeting. After a respectful but reasonable time, we left.

Day at Leisure: Saturday, January 7

Another day of fun in the making. In the morning, I got out my dominoes and other phonics games. Some students were mastering the concepts and vocabulary, but others are too new to it. At least I was happy when a young girl could place the tiles right side up.

In the afternoon I wrote out 2 Timothy 3:16–17 in both English and Spanish. I shared the English with several children, who did not know it (scripture inspired to teach and correct). Joe came along, and after I wrote 1 Thessalonians 5:16–18 (pray without ceasing; be thankful; be cheerful), he copied it all. I helped him with the Spanish, as well as the English. I also got out the New Revised Standard Version (NRSV) to compare the different translations of the passages.

After dinner—chicken and spicy potatoes and plantain (*no rice!*) —I again went to see the men play soccer. After curfew I let whoever came look at the short vowel words and insisted they say the word, rather than just the letters. I got out my flip book to show "fin." Then they wanted to see the rest of the picture book. Movie time came, so most went to see it.

I went to the meeting area with its one ceiling light so as to be alone with my book. Soon a little girl came to be caressed. I read her Philippians 4, about rejoicing. In no time, there were others. I had read several times recently how Jesus was moved with compassion upon seeing the crowds and never understood it. Today I felt the same way as Jesus. When Rufie, the terror from next door, also came (I thought he was a girl once when we played soccer of sorts), I started singing songs with hand motions. He fell right in. My mother would say his energy had to be channeled. I also taught the donkey song: "Sweetly Sings the Donkey." Hands must be on the desk at all times so that the rump is the only thing that jumps at the "hee-haw" time. It was all quite the exhibition in front of Sis Martha and George. I hope they didn't want to confer. ("Sweetly sings the donkey at the break of day./ If you do not feed him, he will run away./ Hee-haw, hee-haw, <u>hee-haw, hee-haw, hee-haw</u>." The underlined part is done quickly.)

Sunday, January 8

My watch wasn't working right. The service began forty-five minutes early, yet everyone was in place. I got to sing most of the Gloria Patri, but the rest was a blur. The hymn books are so old and dilapidated, many pages are missing. I offered to give them a poster of name, service time, and preacher. Now I must follow through.

I have agreed to sponsor a worker and her seven-year-old daughter to come to live in the United States. To make it palatable for Sister Martha, I also agreed to sponsor a twenty-year-old high school graduate and put her through college. She wants to study business management. There are excellent schools for that in Philadelphia. I may have to change my living arrangement, but God will provide.

The younger children got a taste of "The Bunny Hop." This dance wears me out quickly, so after a round of the other songs and dances (La Raspa), I was too weary for much else.

Polly Riddle

Day 15: Monday, January 9

I'm really at Day 12 or so in my folders, but I have an extra two weeks to get to Day 20. I got up thinking it was the middle of the night, but it was really 6:20. The fire was going in the cooking shed, so I got up. It was "wash my jeans and nightgown" day, as well as blouse and undies.

I asked the men, all readers, whether the word *moved* should be a predicate adjective or the second part of a verb phrase in "He was moved with compassion." The consensus was as PA, but some liked the other. I listed it as PA I gave them a review of prefixes and suffixes, with *-ject* and *–act-/tract* as examples. Zaccheaus (Luke 19:1–10) was the Bible study.

I made the sign for the church and then asked the Zion minister if he'd like one. Yes! he said, and asked for it in red. Now I have both men's names and churches: St. Luke United Methodist Church, Service 11:00, Reverend Urias C. A. Pappoe and Trumpet of Zion House of God Church, Sunday School 10:00, Divine Worship Service 11:00, Evangelist/Pastor Joseph C. Jattah. They both have added meaning to my work.

The women didn't show up. Those who work for Sister Martha had to supervise clothes washing. Some of the children worked on my phonics cards. They're getting good.

After dinner—big beans and chicken over rice—I led a Bible study on Mark, introducing it and sharing salient features: (1) *immediate* synonyms; (2) that it was written because witnesses were dying; (3) a little info now, a little more later. It seemed well-received. I will have six days of this.

Day 16: Tuesday, January 10

I got interested in copying the pages of the tablet for the book I will write after this diary. I still have a few to go. Two sets of readers came by to see what I was teaching—*form*, *-mit*, regular verbs in past tense, and Peter's denial (Luke 22:54–65), complete with a picture of a courtyard. I had three women come, all workers with Sister Martha. We got them through subtraction and will start multiplication.

While I was eating dinner—chicken pieces over rice—the men and young men were cutting and shaping the long green bamboo poles to create more clothesline space. The sixty children have lots of laundry. I envied the ones who chinned themselves; how strong they and the poles were!

We had prayer time at six. We prayed for the people being sworn in at the inaugural on January 16. Ellen Sirleaf returns as president. We prayed for the orphanage—funds, staff, and children, especially the ones who still need to commit themselves to the Lord. My safe return to Monrovia and to the United States was part of it. I prayed, too, for the people of White Plains, that their economy would get brighter. It was a former transportation hub and farm area. Now there were few animals and no goods to be transported.

Day 17: Wednesday, January 11

George returned from two days' absence. I brought him up to speed on all he'd missed, as I had copied everything in my notebook. Peter, a teacher here, enjoyed seeing most of the review. He added to the study of the Emmaus Road appearance (Luke 24:13–35).

Kamah came for the women. I also caught her up on a few things. To both George and Kamah, I gave the underpinnings for multiplication. I'd taught her a bit before, but she really ate it up today, even to carrying.

For the second night of Bible study, I finished in the middle of Mark 3. What fun to explain the scriptures! After dismissing the participants, I got a real surprise. Marinda came to see how I was doing and also to discuss finances. Compassion Corps needs receipts for my expenditures, but there really are none. I suggested $100 a week and all the taxi fares. That sounded right.

Day 18: Thursday, January 12

Marinda and Sister Martha joined me for breakfast. I broached the subject of my decision to take three people to the United States and finally admitted that while I might pay tuition, I could not afford room and board while I stayed at my senior residence. I'd have to move. After more discussion, I said there were two phrases rattling around my brain:

"Liberians helping Liberians" and "brain drain." The student could get her business management degree near White Plains and help with the dream the orphanage has. I would also be remiss in allowing a low-wage earner into the United States while she was a teacher and was needed more here. I thus renounced my promise for all three. I could use the airfare money more wisely by applying it to their dream. Both Marinda and Sister Martha were pleased.

Marinda saw a stopped taxi nearby and commandeered it to return her to her place. She'd found out how I was, brought goodies that I'd promptly given to Sister Martha, counseled me, and seen the school, all in twelve hours. What a whirlwind!

I prepared my boards for George: affixes for *-dict* and *tend*. We reviewed irregular verbs and transportation items. I was glad I'd written the latter on the tablet in Monrovia. Luke 23, the death and burial of Jesus, was the scripture.

When I repeated it all for Peter, this august English teacher, his reaction was to say, "He really died." I told him I'd read much about the critics who said he didn't. Others say that the disciples would not have lived and been martyred for a thirty-year hoax.

First one and then three more women got the above in the afternoon, including multiplication. It was heady stuff for them to think they were now multiplying. I taught them how to use the chart for the facts.

After dinner—chicken stew over rice—I helped some youth study for their exams the next week. I found out that Liberia has vast forests, whose felled trees go to other countries for sawing. They could start a tour industry to show the native birds and animals. The pygmy hippo is found only in Liberia.

After a bit of fun and exercise at the soccer venue, I helped Prince, whose uncle had paid his tuition to enter school, albeit the fifth grade at age fourteen. It was a God-thing that I saw my noun poster and put it up. I didn't use it, but the orphan students came by and soaked up its contents. They had just been introduced in their English classes to nouns. The planned days of my lessons will be ending, but I will be here to help the youths study. I'll see more snapshots of what they are learning.

Day 19: Friday, January 13

Today I taught from the noun poster, adding the concepts *common* and *proper*. Peter, the English teacher, came for his lesson. I'd already taught George. I gave Peter a smaller noun poster and a *y-rule* poster. We read about the unbelief of the men at the resurrection in Luke 24—neither the women's tale nor of the rising itself.

The two women in the afternoon knew about men not believing the women. I taught them what I taught George. Kamah was especially receptive. One of the girls asked about a word, *boredom,* from the noun poster; she didn't know the word. When I explained it, she gave a knowing look, as if she had experienced such a thing. I smiled back, knowing about boredom, also.

Teachers Peter and Michael told me they wanted to bring the tenth through twelfth graders over on the Thursday before I leave on the twenty-seventh. There would be pictures of the tablet pages taken, and I would have an opportunity to have a Bible study just for them. I should please write a bio, he said, and include why I'm here and what I've done. He requested that I do it on one page. So I did. I was amazed I could do it so succinctly, another God thing. (It became the preface of this diary, with modifications.)

At night, Sis Martha said she wanted all the kids to be involved in one celebration to honor me. She liked my bio. I let those in charge figure out the details on how to give me honor. My presence has inspired them more than anything I have done. I'm to be taken "downtown" on Saturday. In five or six weeks, I've walked only fifteen minutes away to a church and a soccer field.

Market/Downtown: Saturday, January 14

I thought downtown would be in White Plains, but we actually went to a market, the Red Light Shopping District in Painesville, in the outskirts of Monrovia, and then the heart of the city of Monrovia. I told someone that when I think of a "red-light district," I don't think of a center where any item or service can be obtained. This market was huge and caused traffic jams.

The first leg began around eight thirty in the morning, when we entered the Liberian taxi. Many were hailing a taxi, so ours became full immediately. There was Sis Martha in the backseat, with Prince and me in the bucket seat on the passenger side. A young boy joined the driver for a bit. Sis Martha was joined by two women, one of whom had a baby, and a teen man. After we got out at the market, I took advantage of a photo-op. We walked from one end of the market to the other end and found a taxi going our way. I'd seen wheelbarrows, stands, stalls, blankets on the ground, and people—all with goods to sell. People crossed the street, dodging cars and whatever was trying to move.

In the second taxi, a big lady presided in the front seat, and we three sat in the back seat with a young man. He got out and was replaced three times, not even letting us spread out. It was laughable. Downtown at last! We went to a pharmacy, and while we waited for the prescription, we walked to a post office for a postcard. They didn't have one; only the main one did. We returned to the pharmacy for the pills and went to a watch repair shop. That accomplished, we trekked to the main post office for the postcard. After waiting awhile, we were told the man in charge of postcards had gone for the day, starting his holiday for Monday's inaugural a bit early.

After a small hike through warrens of shops, we got to a restaurant and shared two plates of rice and trout. I enjoyed the green cotton tablecloths, which matched the curtains. I used the bathroom but couldn't figure out how to get the water from the barrel to flush the toilet. Someone else would figure it out. We then found a taxi to return us to the Red Light District Shopping Center. The driver enjoyed using his horn to warn the other drivers he was there.

Sister Martha had a lot of errands at this place. We followed her; I was in the center, with Prince in the back. It was crowded, walking between stalls and real stores in buildings, but we managed. We went into the dark "butchered-animals" market and bought "parts." We visited the woodworking factory where my vanity shelf came from. Sis Martha ordered beds for the new dormitory. Prince and I were sent home in the same taxi that took us; Sis Martha would return in a pickup truck with her treasures. Prince carried all purchases; that was the reason he had come along. Shopping certainly beat an ordinary Saturday at the orphanage.

Sunday, January 15

I decided to wear my orange dress that had the dashiki design. I even let some of the girls fix the hat piece. One had loved to feel my hair the night before and jumped at the chance. They did a super job, of course. Dressed like a lady, notwithstanding socks and sneakers, I sat in my chair and let the children crowd around me. We sang all the songs we knew.

On the way to church, I saw the progress of a new road being cut perpendicular to our road, which now has fewer ruts. The new road was quite near the UN water plant, and I was curious to know where it went. I was told it is a shortcut to the main road to Monrovia.

At church I gave my marquee piece to the pastor and got his picture. It needed to be cut straighter, so we would see if it was put up before I left in twelve days. I told him after worship that it was my last service there; I'd been invited elsewhere the following week. Too involved with pressing money needs, he said only, "Okay." He'd preached a sermon on Malachi 3, "Will a man rob God?"

After dinner Joe came with some geometry equations that I was able to explain, barely. I thought of how Ira would have relished it. After a brief devotional period, most went to see a video, and I to read my *Selecciones del Reader's Digest*. I have one more with me.

Inauguration Day: Monday, January 16

Ellen Sirleaf was sworn in as president of Liberia for the second time. She still stressed education as the best hope for the country. More schools and teachers were being provided. Sister Martha was allotted four from the public sector for her private school, which caters to the town.

We saw it all, kind of, on our TV. Either the TV needed help, or the station needed to improve its feed. I rarely saw color. The swearing-in took place at the University of Monrovia, which we'd passed in our taxi the day before. There was a post obscuring the view of the speakers and singers. I did not see the actual swearing-in, but at least they trained the cameras on her as she gave her speech. The cameras gave us more scenes of the crowd than of the main speakers. We saw important people as they came up to congratulate the president and vice-president.

The young children, who needed some attention they were used to getting from me, then took me for a walk. I wasn't always sure where they wanted to take me, but I was amenable and alerted Sis Martha to our leaving. They wanted to see the UN walkways. Someone at the water plant was accommodating to show it around. We from the orphanage went along a narrow walk between two ponds of water. Even though it had good railings, some younger ones held back. We older walkers finally got them to trust themselves. We then walked down some steps. I hadn't been around this bend, so I was happy to see it all. There was also a tree that had lost most of its leaves off the branches. It seemed strange to see branches without leaves. Granted, in the United States, that's the way it is. This tree had round grey branches that curled. We also saw that the marquee poster was up at St. Luke. It was on the left side; I'd always envisioned it on the right side.

In the morning, before being glued to the TV, I had made six squares each of the numerals 1, 2, 3, 4, 5, and 6, so that I could work a difficult number puzzle like Sudoku. I had it almost worked but had to get the kinks out. I put it away for after the ceremony. Then the walk came, and the older ones needed tutoring for their upcoming exams. The puzzle went on hold. I was finally learning about Liberia from the tutoring I was doing. I also got out my maps to show the students where their country is and where mine is.

After dinner—fish over rice—I led more of the study of Mark, completing chapter four. Then there was more tutoring. Prince needed counseling on not worrying about failing his fifth grade math test; everyone knew he had just arrived and needed more time to catch up. He should persevere and learn it all by June. I couldn't teach him hard fractions until he got through easy multiplication and knew his facts.

Day 19: Tuesday, January 17

George came, and I copied for him the clothing and occupation pages. I don't know what he is learning, but something is going on. I read from John 21: fishing and "Follow me." Then Peter and William came, both teachers. I invited them in to read the "One Minute CreAction Seminar" I had copied from the book *Action Trumps Everything* by Charles F. Keifer, Leonard A Schlesinger and Paul Brown to talk about employment opportunities. It was a one-page summary of the book.

They both scrambled for paper and pen to write it down. Both are the most interested, along with Michael, in the dream of a cash crop to fund a library and a clinic. I shared sawmills, eco-tourism, and photovoltaic ideas, even Heifer International and Techno-Serve, who help natives prosper.

I finished up with George and the rest and continued working on my number puzzle. He was intrigued, and when I finally solved it, he wanted me to copy it for him. What a fulfilling morning!

Polly Riddle

In the afternoon, Kamah came a little early, so I gave her a few fractions, the "seminar," and started clothing. Zenan came eventually. At math time, I gave a decimal presentation to them. After subtracting with decimals, Zenan looked as if someone had shot her with a ray gun, so stunned was she! What will they do when I offer percent?

Some girls had offered to wash my sneakers and socks after the class, so I took them off. They came later and presented them wet and white. The sun would dry them.

I tutored in the evening. One little girl was studying forces: gravitational, inertial, friction, tension, and two more, but she resisted trying to learn it after a bit. She could very well have been overwhelmed. Still, I couldn't help her when she wasn't helping herself. Prince came by with sound wave info. I could deal with that because of my linguistics training, but I reached my limit with the six tools to help man: pulley, wheel and axle, etc. I know what they do and appreciate them, but I just could not explain it fully at 9:45 at night. Joe was there and smiled. I remember failing to explain it to my junior high English (to Speakers of Other Languages) students long ago, even with pictures.

Day 20: Wednesday, January 18

I got up a little late. Breakfast was served right after I put my wash out. Usually I have time for devotions first, but today they came afterward. Samuel came to help me bring out my things, as he usually does, so we did. Then I hid in my room for a bit.

The Best to the Guest

George was in place when I came out at 8:45. Even Samuel had a seat. I put up the chart of long and short vowels and reviewed what I had tried to do. We went over the food chart and compared my life in the United States with now. They don't have the concept of ice cream, hot dog, cake mix, and hamburger. I got out my maps and showed where the people in Acts 2 were from. Then we read about the birthday of the church. I gave the percent equivalents and copied it for George.

Peter, who had come in for the phonics review but had to leave to teach a class, returned. He went page by page through the notes on the newsprint. He wants my handiwork for the night school. It has to be said again, "God was in those plans." (John in Monrovia had first dibs and took them.)

After lunch I helped Prince with a spelling list—words with affixes. I was teaching him how to study. Kamah came early, as she usually does, so I gave her some advanced work: review of adding and subtracting decimals, and starting multiplication and division. Prince heard it all because he remained by special invitation. Samuel was there, too, trying to sleep; Susan, age five, was hitting him, and I finally shooed her away from him, telling her to leave him alone. She left.

By this time two other women came; we looked at the occupation and food charts, Pentecost (Acts 2:1–10), and a review of decimals so as to present percent. It made a good ending. I had taught all my charts.

Two girls, while I was teaching the women, cleaned my room—tiles, toilet, and floor. They had a lot of sweeping under the bed to do. After they knotted all my plastic bags, I asked them to unknot them. My fingers couldn't undo them. Of course they made my bed so that I couldn't tell what was the head or foot; it was time to change it anyway to give me different foam configurations. They straightened stuff that I had strategically placed; the water pails were filled to the brim and sealed tightly with their lids. I asked one girl to undo a bucket so that I would not spill and splash water when I opened it. The mirror was sparkling, and the toilet, tile, and linoleum immaculate. What a good job they had done!

After dinner—chicken and spicy something over rice—I walked for a bit. Nothing was happening in the soccer field, so I returned to prepare the Bible study. The writer of Mark is laying a case for who Jesus is/was. We studied the fifth and sixth chapters and stopped when I could no longer see to read, about seven.

I then helped Prince with more English notes, using a handy flashlight. Another needed help in science. Finally, another whose handwriting I couldn't read could read his own. I drew picto- and bar graphs and then saw that he had his own. I realized it was not me that he needed but my flashlight. Marinda had given me two, so he took the better one, and I went to bed with the other.

Thursday, January 19

At breakfast I gave a pen away. Girls swarmed, and I gave away a few more. I said *no* to one who came later. When I was writing my notes, others came, including the "no" girl. I asked her if she would see "the girl who wanted one but was afraid to ask." I gave her and the other gal a pen, and all who were there at that point. I never should have given to the first one. Many were choosing pink and light teal ink, which may not be acceptable for exams. Pretty, though.

I tried to play the phonics games after lunch, but many were not focusing, and I was out of sorts. I put them away and took a time out. It was better than sending everyone else to their rooms. George had come in the morning; I read Mark to him with commentary for two hours.

After dinner I went with William Moore, the science teacher, and Peter Sennah, the English teacher, to a bend in the St. Paul River. Since it is the dry season, I could see beautiful grass and muddy craters. At the beginning of the rainy season at the end of March or beginning of April, it all floods. Birds use it as a flyover and rest stop. There are lots of fish to catch. Daniel, who lives nearby, showed us around. We saw his burned banana trees, which will regenerate for next year's crop. He also had cassava, pineapples, and sugarcane. The men want me to write a letter to some conservation organizations to see if these could be saved and utilized better. (I did write the letters, but the organizations could not help.)

I didn't quite make it back to the compound before the intestinal flu started. It continued all night into the morning.

Friday, January 20

I requested just tea and crackers for breakfast. They also prepared a nice boiled egg. Yum! I told Sister Martha I had been eating too much fried food and sugar water. It was unfortunate they had to change the sheets again after only one day. Gratefully, Sister Martha gave me a Pepcid tablet, which seemed to stop my problems. I slept all morning and, after lunch, half the afternoon. By two thirty, I was able to play with one person, keeping the others at bay. Then I could play dominoes with the gang.

After dinner—chicken and potato stew (I think they called it soup)—I helped Joe with more Spanish and went out to the soccer field where a game was going on. It was good to stretch the muscles. Back in the compound, I sang and danced with a few children. At night we discovered my new tablecloth glowed in the dark.

Saturday, January 21

At my verandah post while drinking my tea, I saw all the activity to make the compound clean. I see it every day, of course, but sometimes it is abbreviated when the girls are in uniform and getting ready for school. There is a lot of scurrying back and forth. While one is moving desks and mopping the meeting floor, another is mopping the verandah/porch, while another cleans the TV room, where they serve a lot of food. Meanwhile, the sweeper of the courtyard moves leaves and paper to a central area, raising dust that surely gets on the clothes on the bamboo clothesline. Papers and wrappers should not be there, but it is habitual for Liberians to throw their trash on the ground. Someone else will pick it up. I've seen them put the debris on a tin roof piece and take it to the trash heap.

We played phonics games a lot. The little ones took me for a walk. Noting their absence later on, I read some of the conservative Christian Aid Ministry literature. Play was encouraged for the little ones but not sports for anyone; one can get carried away with it for sure.

At night one teen was giving me a shoulder rub. At the end, when my snack appeared, there were six children doing shoulder and hair ministrations. It really felt good. I know when I drink tea, I will have to get up at night.

Sunday, January 22

While some older children and adults went to St. Luke UMC, especially the choir, the younger children and most adults attended the Zion Church, where they honored me with pretty words, a beautiful dress, flowers, and a blessing. I really haven't done anything much for the community, but they seem inspired by my presence. They will go to the night school that will be formed. The dress has purple scallops at the hem and also on the sleeves; the bodice has green rows of scallops in two dovetailing patterns. After I held the flowers—cuttings from shrubs, really—for a few seconds, they were taken away; I never got them back. Little did they know how few times I had received a bouquet of flowers and treasured them. I understood "go" and "return" in the prayer, so I know they wanted me safe.

In the evening, after a fun afternoon, something caught in little Susan's throat. She died in the taxi on the way to Monrovia. The nearer hospitals refused her admission. It is my opinion that even if there were a state–of-the-art hospital next door, they would not have saved her. She was too far gone. After she left, there was spontaneous fervent prayer on her behalf, which lasted about ten minutes. She was in God's hands. That afternoon Prince and I had studied about Jesus, that he had come to heal.

Grief Day: Monday, January 23

We heard of Susan's death early this morning. It was hard to reconcile death in someone so young. Job's response to his children's loss was "blessed be the name of the Lord." The apostle Paul wasn't sure whether he wanted to live or die; to die meant going to a better place.

Susan actually died of an infection in her throat that prevented her from breathing. If she had told someone about her discomfort earlier, she probably would have lived. As a consequence and in the absence of Sister Martha, after dinner many children came to me to show their scrapes and bumps. They had seen my ointments and Band-Aids. One teen had a sore under her ankle; her foot was so dirty I had to soak it before I washed it. I never promised delicacy. (Others had smaller sores and could be disinfected with my hand sanitizer, anointed with Neosporin, and given a Band-Aid.) I'd asked for a clean drying towel, and someone brought me an old skirt. Good enough! I got my soap and smaller bucket for rinsing. Someone brought me a rubber glove since I'd be dealing with blood. The girl gasped at times when I went over her sore spots, but I cleaned with a vengeance, rinsed, and dried it. Then I could sanitize, anoint, and apply Band-Aids. Unfortunately, the last came off as soon as she left. Nothing was totally dry. I told her about "overkill" and wrapped an Ace bandage over the new Band-Aids. Surprisingly, she could get into her flip-flops (in Liberia called slippers). Another girl also got the overkill treatment, and I gave her my airplane socks.

During the morning hours, the place was somber. When I hung out my wash, I confirmed the death. I asked yes-or-no questions and got a nod. I couldn't speak either. I went back to my room for my devotions and cried. I ate breakfast knowing I needed all my strength. I brought out my big Bible and turned to Job. My New Testament was turned to John 11 (Lazarus) and John 14 (no trouble, no orphans, but peace). I even turned to 1 Corinthians 15, and Prince's sister slogged through all of Paul's reasoning about death and rising again: "Death, where is thy victory?" One borrowed my New Testament, so I went to my room for two more. The reading was interspersed with phonics games. We had lost a playmate, so we played. The girl who died, SuLah, wasn't the girl I had in mind at first. I did a double-take when I saw Susan, the one I thought had died.

Pastor Jallah, the UN men, and others from the community came by. A formal mourning area was set up so that Sis Martha and the workers and any children could sit. My place was an alternative in view of the formal area.

By mid-afternoon, I needed time to regroup and went to my room. Then I went out of the compound to see any happenings. A few children followed, and we stretched and danced a bit. The funeral, I found, would be private on Tuesday. There was no school on Monday or Tuesday; in fact, the rest of the exams were canceled.

Bible study took place at five. When I talked about John the Baptist's death by Herod and the healing of the daughter of the Greek woman, I helped put our prayers and mourning in perspective. Our prayers are not answered necessarily by what we want.

Burial: Tuesday, January 24

SuLah, age eight, was laid out in the corner of the boys' dormitory. It may have been the classroom where I spoke to the teenagers at Christmas time. I dressed in my newly gifted outfit and went over. I was too late for Pastor Jallah's service. Soon the chalkboard on which SuLah was to be lain was brought out, and the sheeted and blanketed body was placed lovingly on the board. She was borne by four men past the UN barracks and up the new road. In the states there would have been a motorcade. We walked. Soon there was a turn to the right into a place with other slabs. Two shovels and a pickaxe covered the hole that had been dug.

Two men spoke and lamented. They dropped money into the hole and then got into the hole themselves to receive the body. She was placed lovingly in their care. They got out of the hole and started digging the dirt pile to fill it up. It was time for us to go. I stayed for awhile at the dorm until I realized I should go.

The children needed the domino game. At first, I held a player in my lap, and then I left her in my chair. Soon they stopped the game, realizing I had been bringing order to the proceedings. The smaller children didn't play after that. I would be leaving on Friday, so they had to learn to play by themselves.

After lunch I held court with the wounded. I used my last two Band-Aids with the girl whose sore was under her ankle. Two boys had been hurt while tending the fires. I could only sterilize with hand sanitizer and put on Neosporin. A girl wanted ministrations for an older wound, but I could only do the two things for her. Alcohol hurts on a sore, and they gasped as I applied the sanitizer. I told them it was time for the "Howlelujah Chorus." They didn't get my pun, so eventually I sang a few bars of the "Hallelujah Chorus;" they still didn't get it, but I was having fun. I played dominoes for a bit, but the TV was on. I got to read. Mourners came over to the porch with Sister Martha. After a nap, I read. Mourning took many forms all during the day.

One girl got me to sing and dance with her.

After a surf and turf dinner—three crawdads and a chicken wing over rice; I haven't had any green veggies lately—there was a prayer meeting. Pastor Jallah came to give them a pep talk about being the future of Liberia and then blessed us all with oil, including me. As I returned to my verandah spot, I blessed him too, though without the oil.

Sister Martha told me that electricity was returning to White Plains. We will rejoice. The electric lines were coming right through where the girls' dorm and cooking areas of the orphanage were now; the compound must move. We will rejoice: the new buildings would include power and sockets for the twenty-first century. Yes, moving would be traumatic and costly. The Lord will provide. (The United Methodist compound housed them for nine months until Compassion Corps could build next to the boys' dorm.)

Day at Leisure: Wednesday, January 25

It took a while for me to rationalize why I should get up. There was no purpose for the day. Then I got up because it was the thing to do.

After my devotions and breakfast—cornmeal wedge and hot tea—the children wanted the domino game; we played our requisite three rounds. Prince came over, and for the rest of the morning we did math. His friend came, too. I reviewed them in multiplication and subtraction. They needed to know the facts better, but the tables in their composition book would help them. I also introduced easy division. Joe came to re-copy the Spanish verses; his teacher had been so delighted with it that he had been given it.

In the afternoon, Prince wanted to learn the Spanish verse and copied it. I helped him. He got confused with some of the words, and I worked on English cognates. Cognates look alike in both languages because they are descended from Latin; they work if the English word is known. Prince did not know the fancy words I gave. *Reprehensible* isn't in my ready word bank, either. It was how I described the death of the little girl. The Spanish word for "pointing out mistakes" is *represión* (2 Timothy 3:16). *Comprehension* and *apprehend* (King James Version of Philippians 3:12) come from the same root. *Comprender* and *aprender*, to understand and to learn, are common Spanish verbs, but perhaps *reprender* is less common.

The smaller children resumed dominoes without me after Prince left for lunch. We had a little time for singing and dancing and playing before dinner—greens and crawdads over rice. While waiting for dinner, I observed the repair of the generator; the older boys were enthralled.

My dinner wasn't quite over when the music that rallied the people to the Bible study began. I finished, got my earrings on, and picked up my Bible gear. This was my last chance to present Mark's case for who Jesus was. I reminded the students of several incidents where Jesus claimed to be God. I went on to the transfiguration and the cross; everyone in Palestine knew it, whether they admitted it or not. I concluded with the two greatest commands: love God and love your neighbor (Mark 12. Luke 10 has the Good Samaritan story). It was humbling for me to do this. God was truly in it. The little ones both interfered and helped me get my head together. Yes, it was worth getting up for this day.

Farewell Celebration: Thursday, January 26

Before the hoopla began, I read a magazine in my room. I came out at ten forty, when I heard the children singing what I had taught them. There was a chair especially for me, the honoree. The actual program didn't begin until eleven fifteen. Balloons festooned the meeting area. I'd seen the girls at my breakfast time clearing the desks out, cleaning the floor, and bringing in chairs.

Rufie, whom I had called a terror and thought was a girl, came clad in a dress shirt. I decided the best place for him would be my lap, and there he stayed very well. It was the best place to be. Sis Martha sat in the chair next to me and held another wee one, son of a worker. Rufie is the grandson of a worker.

Pastor Jallah began the official program with a prayer; however, the group had been called to order by the traditional clapping songs. The noise cleared the dogs from the room.

Speeches, songs, and gifts were the order of the day. Peter Senneh, who is in charge of the school, spoke eloquently on my diligence. William Moore, science teacher, spoke on my interest in the "fish pond," the St. Paul River area that overflows in the rainy season. The school and workers gave me three Liberian dresses! I was almost overcome with all of this, but I knew I had to say something. Senneh had said we'd be five thousand miles apart. I said five thousand doesn't seem so far when hearts live and love in Jesus. (John Wesley had said, "If your heart is as my heart, give me your hand.") I said thank you and you're welcome. The Liberian National Anthem was sung, and the benediction prayer was offered by Pastor Jallah.

After lunch, which included papaya, the little ones took me to take a photo of the marquee I'd made for St. Luke UMC. We stopped off at the UN compound (where water is purified for use in Monrovia and all of Liberia) for a picture. Guess what! No more film. The roll that had barely started on Monday had been completely used up. I raced back for more. That gave time for the men to group themselves and the children so that no secrets would be revealed. The picture was already composed when I returned. The men from many countries took more pictures from their cameras. They couldn't see their own children but acted as surrogate fathers to the orphan children. (Already some of these men are being sent home. When I returned a year later, all of the plant was in Liberian hands.)

We finally got to St. Luke. On the way, I noticed the stakes in the new road. We also met George, who returned with us. I got my photo, complete with George the sexton and the children. I'm not sure whether they got water from the church or not. George had unlocked the doors for their getting church water, but I hurried them on. They could get water at home.

I let the people play dominoes by themselves. I was present at first and then sat with others. An older boy was playing with the girls, who were helping him. I think he was enjoying the female attention. He could have left after each game but didn't.

After dinner—surf and turf with greens over rice—I enjoyed the music of choir practice. It got boring too, but there was something soothing to my breast that kept me planted at my seat.

Children came and went into the TV room. I went into the meeting room where I could read by the bulb. Soon the adults were exercising. I had another child on my lap for awhile. I hugged the women and shook hands with Joe, then I retired to my room.

Transition Day: Friday, January 27

My last day in White Plains. I finished packing in stages. The big duffel was stuffed. The tween girls helped me put the boards and newsprint tablet into the big box. Most games had been given to Sister Martha. She played the phonics domino game and was pleased to see them matching grass to grill, flush to flag, plunger to planet. Phonemic awareness had begun.

Polly Riddle

Lunch of fried plantains was the same as what I'd had seven weeks before, when I came late in the evening. It was kind of a full circle. My clothes were declared dry and packed. Marinda came at two, not in a taxi, but in her son John's huge car. Her grandchildren, Denise and Charles Jr., were with her. The son's driver was part of the package. The box had to be at an angle in the trunk, and the bag was on end, but they got in. Sis Martha and two workers came in also to give directions and get a trip to the Red Light Shopping District.

The market was so busy that we had to wait a long time for traffic to smooth out; we finally got going again. When we went off New Georgia Road, I was asked if I knew where we were. Yes, I did. I had walked in these shortcuts and ridden in the lanes. I might have missed a turn once, but I immediately righted myself. The school/house compound with its five-foot cement wall was a welcome sight. I had enjoyed the bamboo-fenced compound, but this was home with Marinda.

After dinner—greens and chicken over rice, eaten with Marinda and served with ladles—we plotted how my time would be used: ten days phonics and math in the morning for both sexes and a literary study of Mark from three to five. Rebecca came to say hi.

There was time also to see the new basketball backboards. Some of the family were playing, so I got up on the court and made a lucky basket. I'd been taught how to make a free throw, but it had been a long time.

Day at Leisure: Saturday, January 28

I read part of a book about the settlement of East Liberia by the Gedebo, or Kleo. Its founders were Yawah Toe and the most important Paramount Chief WreaMusu. The authors William K. K. Reeves and Alphonsus G. N. Davis are their descendants. Marinda is Kleo.

Tired of reading, I unpacked my box and set up my easels. I was now ready for Day 1 on Monday. It was good to sort out my supplies.

Marinda and I were to be off for a clinic after a cracker lunch, but a person came to put in the door to her office. Thus, we stuck around for two hours. She napped on her couch, and I read the primers and kindergarten math booklets on her desk. I disagreed with some of the teaching strategies and saw correctable errors; it passed the time. Dinner was ready, so we sat to eat our potato greens and chicken over rice.

Finally, we were off. We walked to New Georgia Road

Sunday, January 29

I dressed for church in the dress I'd been given the previous Sunday. Of course, I was the first to arrive. The other women had to cook breakfast, clean the floors, and dress the children. Soon it was eleven in the sanctuary, the school auditorium. Two males started the music until the females got there. I'd been enjoying the drums but also appreciated the shaker beat, singing, and chanting.

I gave my testimony of praise that I had been given two more weeks there since the third place couldn't take me: there was more opportunity to teach. The sermon was from Exodus 14: do not be afraid, stand still, see the salvation of the Lord, and go forward. While I missed hearing about the last part, I was assured it was there. When they asked me to bless the offering, I prayed about the loaves and fish that were few but in the hands of Jesus fed five thousand. The money should be so blessed.

Dress off and T-shirt on, I ate, finished reading the book on Liberia, and watched the basketball playing. Charles, the preacher and Marinda's son-in-law, had learned to play well before the war; now he taught the youngsters what he knew. There were two basketballs going, one for each end.

Since Marinda had been delayed getting home from the clinic for her third injection, I was late in eating. By six forty-five, I was faint. Charles and Genevieve were eating but didn't seem to worry about me. They were enjoying their food at the flagpole so that they could enjoy the basketball, too. I finally asked them if there was provision for me. It had been served at my usual place, just not communicated to me. What a breach of guest relations! I served my plate and ate outside, too. I'd been given a comfortable chair. In the evening the cousins got me to read from Dr. Seuss.

Polly Riddle

Day 1: Monday, January 30

All my former students whom I had taught to read showed up: Nathaniel, Rebecca, Lucy, and Tenneh. We studied rich-man stories in Luke 16 and 17. To end the class, I gave them fancy words in fractions: numerator, denominator, proper, improper, and mixed number. We raised numbers to higher terms and tried to find common denominators. I wanted them in the afternoon class.

Lunch, laziness, and restlessness described me. I finally went to the auditorium where I would be teaching and wrote the outline for John the Baptist, put down the compare and contrast forms for Jesus and John, and generally prayed. No one arrived at three, but Pastor Charles, Marcus, Rebecca, Seba, and her husband, Samuel, eventually sauntered in. It was good.

Dinner of yams and chicken over rice was laid out, so I ate. Marinda was on day four of five daily injections to help arthritis in her hand. I found a chair at the "end zone" of the basketball court and watched the play. Marinda came and encouraged me to take a picture of it. She then took me to her newly-made bookstore and upstairs to see the new doors for all the classrooms. The evening ended with my reading two Dr. Seuss stories to the girl cousins. One fell asleep during the first one, and the second during the second. Abbis, an eleventh grader, was still enjoying the mayhem of the McGrew Zoo from *If I Ran the Zoo*. The girls had been with me during the morning session; I used them to teach compare and contrast.

Day 2: Tuesday, January 31

When Rebecca came again, I put up the outline of John the Baptist and taught what it was. The outline was new learning, even for readers. In came Olivia, who needed to learn from Day 1, so I told her I'd finish the outline and map of Palestine, and then give her exclusive attention. She knew how to write her alphabet and copied the outline. Evelyn, who had come in sporadically last time, also profited from the beginning lesson with Olivia. (Unfortunately, there was so much recess noise at the end neither person returned for lessons.)

The Bible study began at 3:55. The girls from Dr. Seuss fame were there, so I started with them. Soon more came in, most different from the day before. I didn't finish all that I'd planned, but enough. We had story elements from the healing of the paralyzed man, summary of Chapter 1, and redirection: if you don't like others' questions, make your own. Jesus was a master of that. We also touched on rhetoric and metaphor. God answered my prayer to figure out how to deal with old cloth and new wineskins: Jesus brought new ideas; the old way would no longer be sufficient.

After dinner—greens on chicken over rice—the basketball fun was in full force. I'd been given a Liberian history book and finished it. When the generator was on and the TV evident, I escaped to my room with a UMC hymn book I found. Marinda and I sang. She was also looking for something, but I didn't know how to help her. I was invited by Marinda's son John, who works for President Sirleaf, to be honored at lunch the next day for what I'd done. I didn't catch who was doing the honoring.

Day 3: Wednesday, February 1

Neither Olivia nor Evelyn came for lessons. The older cousin profited from the lesson and wrote it down. Rebecca came. I read from *The Wocket in My Pocket* by Dr. Seuss, which I'd read to the cousin. Rebecca wrote it down in her book. Then I got out the third grade social studies book about Liberia. We enjoyed looking at land forms of the country: mountains, hills, lowlands, rivers, lakes, and ocean. When I was called to dinner, I let her take it home, assuming she would like to copy some of it.

The son John, who works in the government and got us an audience with President Sirleaf during my first visit to Liberia, was acting on his own to honor what I was doing. Marinda and I were taken downtown, crossing the newly opened Water Street Bridge that had been destroyed during the civil war.

The driver—the same one in the same car who took me from White Plains to Monrovia—took us to Shirley's Restaurant, where John and his best buddy were just finishing lunch. The friend's wife came in while we were eating. Since I requested a not-so-spicy meal, they grilled fish and gave me French fries. I rarely eat fries in the states but ate a few here. Most of the fries were given to the wife. The fish was good. They also served me vanilla ice cream, which I finished. Yum!

John drove us to a place where the driver could pick us up. Marinda took advantage and was taken to see her niece, who was visiting from Minnesota. She'd been invited to the inaugural. If I'd been in town, I'd have been invited, too. With a trip to the gas station, Marinda's treat, we got home.

It was after three in the afternoon, but only John from Scripture Union was at the Bible study. Liberians are known to be late, and I took advantage this time. Soon more people arrived, and I'd written the day's lesson. Mark 4 says we have to keep planting and trusting that there will be a harvest.

The Best to the Guest

Some computers arrived for Marinda, which kept her busy; thus, I invited Rebecca to eat with me. I'd gotten my book back. She'd fallen asleep at one point, possibly from hunger.

At the evening Bible study they were talking about the need for passion to save souls. I was asked to pray aloud for this. I'd heard "Let's pray," but not the "Mama Polly, please pray." James, the son who drove me from the airport, and his wife were with Marinda. Daughter Marie, who catered our dinners in 2010, had come to pick up her three children, the cousins I'd gotten to teach and read to. Lots of love had been shared. What fun to meet four of Marinda's five grown children on one day! (Genevieve lives there.) Another daughter lives far away.

Day 4: Thursday, February 2

I put up my easels, boards, and papers, but at first no one showed up to use them. Rebecca and Tenneh eventually did, and we studied the first unit of the Liberia book. They would profit, and I would be entertained.

Marinda was excited that she had four new computers and three more reconditioned ones. I'm not sure where they came from. Her computer room could be put to use, assuming the generator worked. She would get a new generator when the money came in from my tax refund. She also gave me a dress in the butterfly pattern: serape with sides sewn straight down, six inches from the edge of the cloth. The print shows Ellen Sirleaf and her VP. It also comes with a hat piece. I'll wear it to the farewell party.

I came early, as usual, to do my Bible study boards. The choir practice was going on, but we were compatible since we did not have to pay attention to each other. The choir director and assistant pastor, Samuel, came at three and wanted to start Bible study, so I did. Another fellow came soon after. We dramatized the healing of the demon-possessed man as he came from the tombs. After more people came, we did it again.

After the study, Ben and Steve stayed; they had registered for the eleventh grade but failed the math exam. I gave them an easy division problem, and they stared at it. One could not subtract. I told the brother who could to teach the other. I would see on the next day if they could multiply; I had to teach them about the multiplication tables.

Dinner—boiled potatoes, chicken, and beans over rice—was delicious. The dog, which before I had thought was lazy, had given birth to five puppies. I petted the puppies a bit and put a little water in their bowl. Their care by humans has been minimal, for some of their hair is out where they've scratched and bitten their fleas. Abbis has cared for them.

I studied the lesson of John the Baptist's death and will complete the outline by giving capital letters to Herod, Herodias, daughter, and guard. I debated whether it was amoral or immoral. Only John was moral. Such a sad death.

Day 5: Friday, February 3

Rebecca showed up and picked up the social studies book. We learned about the first peoples that came from Africa: both hunter-gatherers and farmers, as well as *canoers* (I coined this word; yes, the people who came in canoes), all having a language different from English. The former slaves from America in Liberia, called *settlers*, knew only English. There are perhaps ten or more native languages in Liberia. To accommodate the settlers, English became the official language in government, schools, and commerce.

She stopped after an hour and wanted scripture. I read from Matthew 12:43–45, about the demon who came out of the heart of a man and returned to it, now vacant, cleaned, and decorated. He invited seven other devils, too. I said the best way to prevent this was to fill the heart and mind with positives and read from Philippians 4:1–9: be glad, think on good things, be thankful.

After she left, I started drawing a recess crowd. There was little I could do for them, so since there would be an assembly in an hour, I let them help me take down my boards and move them to out-of-the-way spots. I left and washed out three of the long dresses I had worn during the week. I ate lunch early.

Marinda basically twisted my arm to get me to attend assembly with her. The fifth grade was leading it and had invited Josephus, an eleventh grader who wants to be a minister, to speak; "focus and go forward" was his message. I was asked to say a few words and told them about the devils and positive thinking. Marinda piggybacked on the theme, too. I couldn't understand much of what was said, but if my presence could help, I was willing.

The two boys from the day before wanted to be tutored then since they live far away. The subtraction was better. They could divide with errors after a time. I introduced algebraic concepts—commutative, associative, and distributive properties and the Pythagorean theorem with square root; I now had two heads. These were teens I'd come to teach: the war had interrupted their studies. We would get in touch with a lot of ideas the next week.

Returning to the house to rest and get my bag of Bibles, I was given a yogurt treat. Yum! Then it was on to the Bible study. I couldn't get any discussion on whether Herod and his gang were immoral or amoral. The class members didn't seem to care. Chapter 6 of Mark had many highs and lows; I labeled them on a wave pattern as a summary.

My dresses were dry but stiff as boards. Marinda suggested using an iron. Turning them right side out and wearing them would soften them, too. Their iron has hot coals in it.

Dinner was special—palm butter and pumpkin with chicken over rice. Palm nuts are boiled and pounded into butter. It was quite flavorful. It's the favorite of the tribe. Afterward, I watched basketball—an actual game. Lines had been marked to indicate where foul lines should be. I couldn't tell who played whom, but it was exciting to see them all go through their paces. A few spectators sat on the five-foot concrete wall and occasionally stopped the ball from going outside.

There's a five to seven foot space between the concrete slab and wall. Wheelbarrows and people came by to draw water at the pump in the corner. Afterward I walked for exercise on the slab and noted how rough it is in spots. The young men were often barefoot or in flimsy sandals or flip-flops they call slippers. I ended the day singing some hymns from the UMC hymnal and listening to a religious radio broadcast with Marinda.

Day at Leisure: Saturday, February 4

While I took a day off to relax, Marinda went to the markets for shopping. The palm butter seemed to be affecting me, so I was glad I stayed home.

Sister Martha came while Marinda was still away. It was fun to discuss old times and the plans for the move when the electric poles came to take the girls' dorm and cooking area away. They had not then firmed up where they would go, but I later found out the girls and boys were moved to the UM hostel, and a girls' dorm was being built next to the boys' dorm. The boys' dorms, school, and field were not affected. As I was showing off the artwork done by Jen Bucy of St. Andrew's UMC from our time before, in came Marinda. Money had arrived from Compassion Corps for my stay. I was happy to know that this money had now been paid to my hostesses. I still owed a bit and would send it when I returned to the states.

A long-time friend of Pastor Charles came to visit. He now resides in Cameroon with his native wife and four children; he has a church of 150 people. What a missionary effort! He opined on Liberia: developmentally it was better now, but before the war, family cohesiveness was better. With so much killing, the young were too often rootless and therefore independent of family.

In the evening, while basketball was played, Marinda worked at the program in my honor for next Saturday. I helped her transcribe words from the UMC hymnal: #98, "To God Be the Glory" and "America." We finished by lantern light. Others came, and we moved inside. Since Marinda started singing and dancing, I added my Greek snake dance and led the dance La Raspa in a circle with two youngsters. I'm too out of condition (too old?) for much more than two rounds of the Bunny Hop, but I taught it to the tune of "Lord of the Dance."

Sunday, February 5

I dressed in my country cloth dress that Marinda had given me eight weeks previously. It had a kind of dashiki print on it. With a matching headband for a hat, it looked quite fetching. Marinda wore a red-and-blue stole and hat with her white dress. How elegant we were!

Marinda's son-in-law, father of the three cousins who had stayed last week, took us to First UMC of Monrovia. We were late in our schedule for going, but we were on time for the service. I'd had time to take pictures of the dog with her five puppies, now five weeks old.

The service was traditional, complete with organ and enrobed and processional choir. Bishop Bledsoe from North Dallas, Texas, was there for the Liberian annual conference and preached. Bishop Innis of Liberia introduced him. They had on their bishop robes and stoles. The female minister had on a long white dress and white veiled hat with wide brim. I couldn't understand much of what was spoken through the microphones except the sermon topic, spiritual leadership. Marinda said he spoke from Jonah, who was to listen well and obey promptly—good advice for us all. At the end of the service the distinguished entourage posed for their paid photographer. Since I had prayed for such a shot, I went up my three pews and nudged away the photographer after he had taken his photo. The important personages stayed posed for my importunity. I was the only white person at the service and had stood when they called for visitors. After the two-hour service, I gave the minister a New Testament with a dollar bill. They'd had one offering at the seats for their radio broadcast. Another offering was the lineup of members to pay their pledges to the treasurer at the front table. This is such a cash society that checks in an envelope was not totally feasible.

Marie's husband took us (and his older daughter with him) to James, who had taken us from the airport when I arrived, to James's house. I wish I had cornered Marinda to write these names down. He and his wife had invited us to dinner: beef, chicken, collard greens and rice, with ice cream cups for dessert. I even had a Coke, along with a small bottle of water. We watched the video of Ben Carson, how he overcame so much to become a renowned pediatric surgeon. His mother and his wife gave him inspiration. There were captions, so I followed it well.

In the evening, we relaxed. I ate just a little spinach and rice. I figured out some of the plans for the next day. Marinda was so tired she put her head down at the table while listening to her radio program. I gave her a back rub.

Day 6: Monday, February 6

No one showed for class for quite a while. I was able to write the outlines on outlining and John, so now I was ready to teach Marinda's noon classes. I'd arisen late and hadn't had time to read my devotional materials; I had time for that now. After reading from the New Testament a bit, Rebecca and Lucy came in. We read from the social studies book. I also showed them my outlines.

Suddenly it was twelve fifteen. I found Marinda. She gathered the tenth- and eleventh-grade classes from their upper floor, complete with their chairs, to the auditorium. I went over the outline of outlines once or so. Students were still trying to get settled and absorb it. Then Marinda took over and said it again. It was too much info in too short a space, even though it was clear.

I ate a hasty lunch and returned to teach math to my two boys and their friend. They're getting multiplication and division, so I added decimals. One asked me what an axiom was; fifty years after studying geometry, I told him it was a statement taken on faith that it was true. It just wasn't provable. We stake our lives on it. He smiled.

After they left, I quickly put up the literary forms for the Mark study. I contrasted spiritual and physical contamination; I defined repartee, retort, and allegory. I was gratified that I had a few minutes rest, thankful to be useful in God's kingdom plan. Pastor Charles came in, and we talked about contamination in Chapter 7. We moved on to the next topics. Nathaniel came in, but I was glad for the *tête-à-tête*. Charles has appreciated my scholarship of the Jewish culture, which increased his understanding of it. At the end, sans Charles, I read at Nathaniel's pace; we were all pleased at his accomplishment. He was still using the glasses I gave him.

After dinner—chicken, yams, and eggplant over rice—there wasn't too much to do. I tried reading for the next day's lesson and finally hit on a grid for all the repetition in Chapters 9 and 10, with a review of Chapter 8: blind healing, children, death announcement, and greatness versus servanthood. Great themes.

Day 7: Tuesday, February 7

No one came for teaching in the morning. I read a bit from my Spanish commentary, the end of 2 Timothy 2: characteristics of good Christian workers.

Then I noticed the class next door didn't seem to have a teacher and verified it. I went in to see if I could help. They were studying continents, so I asked which one they'd like to know more about. "Europe," said one intrepid boy. I drew a map of Europe and started in with Portugal, Spain, France, Germany, and Italy. Then I talked about paintings in cathedrals, museums, and palaces. Another topic was how vendors in Spain dealt with foreign visitors: they have pictures with prices and show the total amount on their calculators, even changing to dollars or whatever money is necessary. Then I was asked about the United States and showed them the states where I'd lived, beginning in Washington on the Pacific Coast and ending with New Jersey and Pennsylvania. I've also lived in Ohio, Florida, Louisiana, and Alabama. I talked of cold and snow and what I might face when I return.

My undoing may have been the exercises I led them in. Several seemed to be asleep. They finally went to recess. I returned to my classroom, the auditorium, and found three notebook papers hanging by my magnets: "You are the best," "We love you," and "God bless you." I'm not sure who did it, but they will get to the United States. When I returned to this sixth grade class after lunch, they greeted me with gyrations we'd done. I wasn't sure whether they were mocking or praising me. I finally got them to sing to me: "The Star-Spangled Banner," a hymn, and perhaps their national anthem—all seated. What a lively group!

I waited, but my boys were no-shows. Evidently a greater priority had their attention. The clinic manager, Tage, came by. I gave him my Ace bandages, which had been wrapped around my boards and New Testaments. He told me his daughter graduated from nursing school and was now the doctor's assistant. She would be married on March 11. On that day, the groom and his parents come to the bride and her parents to formally ask for her and give a token. When they assent, they give a party; the two would now be married in the eyes of Liberia. The Western wedding in a church can come later, if desired.

No one came to the three o'clock Bible study. Thinking it was Wednesday, at four fifteen I packed up my boards for the next day. I read a bit and then ate alone—spinach and chicken over rice. Some students came over and made it lively while I watched the basketball events. With the students gone, I even got a chance to hit and miss some baskets. Tenneh brought me a grapefruit.

Day 8: Wednesday, February 8

Tenneh's grapefruit was white and sweet inside. In the United States, whites are bitter. I scored it with a butcher knife.

Tenneh and Mamie registered for a night school, took a test, and landed in the seventh grade. While they didn't start totally from scratch from me, I got them over a big hump. They still insist I taught them to read. Rebecca would end up starting in mid-fifth grade at a United Methodist day school; a year later I learned she had passed sixth grade.

Rebecca had found a place in the kitchen here, helping make snacks for the students to buy at recess. I put out the boards with Chapters 8–10 on them, telling Marinda they were from the day before. She found an eighth-grade class that could profit from it. Down the steps the students came with their chairs into my big room. I loved it. An hour or so later, I returned them to their classroom.

The two boys had not come to school at all on Tuesday, so today I worked them until three. They were sagging after fractions and decimals, but they're prime for percents. We worked around the writing on the boards. Nathaniel came in, and Josephus came in for a bit. Since there would be an evening Bible study at five, I erased each board in turn.

Dinner was chicken stew over rice. For a bit of time at the Bible study, only Abbis at the drums and I, keeping rhythm with the drums, were at the service. A few others wandered in and out since the preachers had not arrived. The preachers eventually came together, and I gave Samuel my hundred days of important Bible passages devotional and Charles my study Bible. More household people came and a few outsiders. We learned about spreading the gospel to our Jerusalem—our own friends and community.

After the service, I studied my lesson and decided to make an outline of "Temple Antics" for Chapters 11–13, traps for and teachings of Jesus, with elaborations. Time it was for bed after listening to the radio with Marinda.

Day 9: Thursday, February 9

Pastor Samuel came by to thank me again for his gift book. We talked on what the area "Samaria" might be in the neighborhood around the school and church. At prayer meeting the night before we heard from Acts 1:8 about going to Jerusalem, Samaria, and the rest of the world. The speaker spoke only of Jerusalem, where our friends and those who "look like us" live. *Samaria* would be those places that are despised or who are different; Jesus insisted on going through Samaria on his way to the cross. He healed lepers and spoke to a woman at a well. Samuel and I also spoke about how important it is for ministers in an area to get together to mutually edify, worship, and swap ideas with one another. Had a *ministerium* been in place, it would have been easy to advertize my coming the second time around. Isolation is insidious.

Polly Riddle

At the Haweh recess, I felt like singing and dancing, so I did with a few students. Soon my corner was crowded. The circle dancing La Raspa didn't go around: it went right and then went left. Fun was had by all!

After my usual cheese and crackers lunch, I taught the two boys about per cents and order of operations. I made sure they could multiply and divide by two digits. They still don't know their multiplication facts, but they're good at using the tables.

At four fifteen, I told myself I would wait five more minutes. Within that time, Nathaniel and Josephus wandered in. So did a woman that seemed lost, but she stayed. For Chapters 11–13 I had made an outline called "Temple Antics": testing and teaching, inside and out. It was fun to contrast the triumphal entry to the serious Roman legion show of force happening elsewhere but not recorded in the New Testament.

After dinner—collard greens and chicken over rice—I finally sat with Marinda to show her the bio I'd written and the papers of thanks students had posted. She modified the bio and will use it on Saturday when I'm honored. Abbis brought in two pails of water to the bathroom; since he is strong, he doesn't spill water. I made sure the doors were open so he could sail right through. Otherwise, the water is left at the bedroom door, two doors and two curtains away from its target area.

Instead of class in the auditorium, which Marinda wanted to clean and decorate for the farewell celebration the next day, I went with her to the kindergarten rooms and taught some songs. It held three classes in one room; the Board of Health would not approve. I'm not sure how they got down to their ankles to illustrate the rains coming down (their arms start at the top and move down) in "The Wise Man Built His House upon the Rock," but they did. For "Deep and Wide" we just put palms together instead of a full arm span. They still remembered "Hee Haw" from thirteen weeks earlier. Marinda liked to sing.

Mamie came by, and we sat talking. After lunch I met my two students and taught them on the front porch. We knew from how far they had come and how much they still were shaky on, but I felt confident they would succeed. Nathaniel came. We did only Chapter 14. He wrote my "Mark's Case for Jesus as Son of God" summary, and we and called it good after prayer. It was nearly six.

After dinner—chicken and beans over rice—I watched the basketball doings. The three cousins came, and I read *Dr. Seuss's ABC* book for all who were interested. I'd been contentedly reading from Acts alone.

Saturday, February 11

After the usual cream of wheat, I spent the morning packing. I needed to be out of everyone's hair anyway. It was good to have time to think and decide where everything should go. Would this be Marinda's, John's, or mine to take home?

After my hearty lunch—chicken, potatoes, chickpeas, and the late-arriving rice—I read to the kids and watched the comings and goings. At two, it was time to be dressed. When I returned, I saw that several students had on "Mama Polly" T-shirts; my friends were preparing sandwiches and other delights for refreshments. I used my last photo op to get a picture of me with my students, I in my green butterfly outfit with hat and they in the special T-shirts. (This photo did not come out, as Ben and Steve had brought joy to themselves by taking an entire roll of film, less one photo, of themselves. Nothing was left for photos I wanted.) Sis Martha arrived; she'd spent all night with her chorus and came when they left for home. Marinda had made sure to invite her and recognized her in the program.

We three came in together and sat on the front row. The mistress of ceremonies ticked off each thing in the schedule: singing, a skit on the Good Samaritan (she forgot to call the other skit), recognitions, and prayer. Both the American and Liberian national anthems were sung. I was the only one standing for *The Star-Spangled Banner*. While the roomful of people stood for their anthem, the reporter for the event eventually stood, too.

I stand if everyone else does. The mothers' prayer group I'd installed gave me two tops. The church gave me slippers and a purse. Marinda and her students gave me a huge painting of me with lettering at the bottom. I was overwhelmed! It was painted by a student, Picasso Sawyee.

I didn't have a Picasso at home; now I would. A preacher read Isaiah 60:5–7 (we'll all be together some day). I would read it when I get home. Such an outpouring of love!

Plates of food were again brought to us who were seated. I'm used to going to the food table, but here in Liberia, I have been served at my seat. It is a matter of portion control.

The press person got me outside. Wearing the pretty sandals I was given and walking unsteadily, I was lagging behind John, who finally saw that I was cornered. I was asked to compare schooling here and in the United States. I'm glad I could use Marinda's ideas of privilege. In the United States, pupils often take their education for granted; here in Liberia, it is a privilege. The press man finally went on to other people.

Both of Marinda's sons came after the program was over. Marinda gave me a "Mama Polly" T-shirt (plus shirts for Pastor Wendy, Jan and Beth of Compassion Corps, and my sister Carolyn, whom we had called several times). Lucky me! Sister Martha found my bed immediately after the program. I couldn't budge her when I went to bed, so put the netting around her as best as I could. I slept on my bed where she wasn't. In the middle of the night we righted ourselves.

Sunday, February 12

Sis Martha seized the light that had been on all night and used it to read. I saw the glimmer of light outside and realized I could do my usual morning routine: put up mosquito netting, make the bed, bathroom duties, dress, write in my journal, and read my devotional.

After breakfast I read to the cousins. The girls were treated to new hairdos by Martha and Marinda. Such love! I decided to go to worship on time and let the others be late. My safety was prayed for by Pastor Charles. A guest speaker preached.

After the sermon, I was told to go eat lunch—Marinda's son James, our ride, was here. I changed, ate, and got into the car. My bags got in, too. The boards and things for John had fallen to the floor and stayed there. John and Marinda would sort it all out eventually. The big box stayed. The formerly oversized stuffed bag was now a compact eighteen pounds. My purse was in my small carry-on bag so that the big wooden picture could be my second carry-on.

The three cousins were returned home along the way to the airport. Later on that trek, we had a flat tire. Marinda persuaded a driver of a car that stopped to help to take us to the airport. Reluctantly, he did. Life in Liberia! Just to enter the airport cost 50 Liberian dollars (LD) (US $15), which Marinda paid, whether you stayed five minutes or five hours. Marinda and Martha shared the handle of my bag, not allowing me to haul it. I was still the guest. Denise Alpha, child of Pastor Charles Alpha and Marinda's daughter Genevieve, carried my big picture. I was checked in outside the airport so quickly I didn't have a chance to hug them all one final time. A skycap kindly wrapped the picture to protect it; he enjoyed my tip. Another enjoyed his tip for carrying my bag through the lines.

The planes were on time, with no rough patches worth talking about. Thank you, God. We went back the way we'd come: Monrovia, Liberia to Accra, Ghana, where we stayed on the plane while they cleaned and straightened. Then it was on to Atlanta, Georgia, where we dealt with customs and rechecking bags, always a slow, nerve-wracking experience.

Monday, February 13

In Philly, no one was at the station to meet me. My friends really had not been notified, except for the notice three months previously. Thus I took the train. I learned to drag my bag on one wheel. In Warminster I persuaded a woman to take me home. I was so weak I needed three tries to lift my eighteen-pound bag into a shopping cart.

I signed in at the senior center at 1:00 p.m.—time for ping pong! Life in my senior center in the United States resumed, God be praised!

Appendix A
Gospel of Mark

Outline: John the Baptist (Mark 1, 6)
I. Prologue: Purpose
   A. Prepare the/your way
   B. Make paths straight

II. Birth (Luke 1)

III. Ministry
   A. Message
      1. Repent—change your lives
      2. Be baptized—show change
   B. Personal characteristics
      1. Food: locusts, wild honey
      2. Dress: camel's hair, leather belt
   C. Humility—not worthy to untie sandals of one coming
   D. Baptism of Jesus

IV. Arrest and Death
   A. Herod—guilty conscience
      1. Imprisoned John
      2. Married brother Philip's wife
   B. Herodias—wife of brothers
      1. Hated John
      2. Wanted him killed

Polly Riddle

    C. Daughter
        1. Danced to please
        2. After consulting Mom, asked for John's head on a platter *now*
    D. Guard
        1. Obeyed Herod's order to behead
        2. Presented head on platter

V. Burial: by John's disciples

Synonyms for "as soon as possible"
immediately: at that very moment, at once, right away, then, instantly, suddenly

Compare		Contrast
	John	Jesus
message	Repent, be baptized	Trust Good News Kingdom has come
where from	Judea	Nazareth
wilderness	Voice/ministry	Temptation
voice	As messenger From God	Son
disciples	Fasted With groom	no fasting
type of baptism	Water	Holy Spirit

Triangle of Sonship (Connect Xs to form a triangle)
                X   Transfiguration: Son loved,
                                        Listen to Him

    X Baptism: Loved Son,   X Cross: Centurion –
            God finds happiness   Surely Son of God

Pronunciation:
prophecy (see): Noun prophesy (sigh): Verb   Prophet: person
Mark 1:1 begins case for Jesus Christ as the Son of God

Story elements—Mark 2: 1–12 Forgiveness and Healing

Setting:
    time: daytime
    place: Capernaum home

Characters: crowd, legal experts, four friends, paralyzed man
    Main character: Jesus, paralytic

Plot: A man, paralyzed since birth, helped by friends is healed
    Problem: Room too crowded to bring man in
    Solution: Go through the roof

Themes: perseverance, God forgives and heals, authority, different reactions

Case as Son of God: Positive—can forgive sins as well as heal
    Negative—house divided cannot stand; therefore cannot be from Satan

Synonyms: Son of Man, Son of God, The Human One
mat, bed, cot

Redirection: If you do not like the questions you are asked, then change the perspective by asking your own. Jesus was a master at this.

Summary of Chapter 1: John prepares the Jews for Jesus Christ, Son of God. Jesus, baptized and tempted, becomes so popular because of his healing and demon-removal that he cannot move openly.

Summary of Chapter 2: Jesus heals a man who was paralyzed; he also claims to be God by forgiving the man's sins. He calls Levi, a tax collector, who serves him and his friends a meal. When the religious leaders murmur, Jesus answers that he is called to care for the sick. He is the Groom—no fasting; it's a new day! He is Lord of the Sabbath.

Polly Riddle

Summary of Chapter 3: Do good or evil? Do good on Sabbath. More demons cast out. The twelve chosen and sent out as apostles. Jesus explains why he cannot be from Satan's family; his kingdom is for those who obey him. House divided cannot stand.

Chapter 4: Cause and Effect—Sower went to sow: Farmer cast/scattered seed

Cause	Effect
1. Path was too compact	Birds came and ate
2. Rocks allowed for no roots - too shallow	Dried up
3. Thorns choked the seed sprouts - too tangled	Sprouts strangled
4. Good soil allowed penetration and growth	Produced mature plants

Parable—A story with one main point. In this story the point is that we must plant the seed of the gospel, and at some point it will produce believers.

Chapter 4 Summarization

Parables told and explained. Keep sowing/scattering seed. What you do will be made plain and come back to you at some point. Be aware of what you have; if not, it will be taken away. The Kingdom of God is like a mustard seed. It grows big. Keep planting/working. Jesus has power over wind and sea.

Two healings:

Compare		Contrast
females	Girl	Woman
#12	Age	Years of bleeding
belief	Faith	Trust
promotion	Father Jairus	Self—touch hem

The Best to the Guest

Mark 5:1–20 Sequence, CHARACTERS

Scene 1	JESUS	DEMONS	MAN
At first	Out of boat	Possess man	Out of tombs
Then	"Come out!"	Negotiate	Saw, ran, knelt
After that	Lets demons enter pigs	Enter pigs	As dead
Finally		Run to lake, drown	Sane
Scene 2	TOWNSPEOPLE		
	Notified		
	Come, see man		
	Ask Him to leave		
Scene 3	JESUS		MAN, NOW SANE
	Returns to boat		Wants to come with
	Tells him to return home		Returns to his people
	to tell what He did		Told what was done

Question for application for Mark 5:1–20: What has Jesus done for you that you can share with others?

Summary Chapter 5
Jesus frees a demon-possessed man on one side of the lake. He was asked to leave after he let the demons enter pigs, which drowned. On the other side of the lake he heals a woman, who touched his clothes, and brought back to life a girl of twelve.

Chapter 6 Theme: Excess—too many highs and lows
Highs: *Apostles* returned *Jesus* preaches, **heals 5000 fed Jesus on water**

Lows: John beheaded...*Disciples*...**Too busy to eat**...perplexed...**terrified**

(Draw waves to indicate highs and lows.)

Chapter 7: Contamination.....Contrast

Spiritual	Physical
Of God	Of flesh and body
Heart/mind >good/evil>actions	Dirt/germs/food>skin/mouth>sewer
Hypocrisy/not walking the walk	Does not matter if food is clean or unclean

1. Disobedience to God's commands
2. Empty worship
3. Sin (7:21–22)

Mark 7:24–32 Greek woman's daughter healed

Repartee: trading/sharing retorts
Retort: good answer or comeback
Allegory: elements mean something else

>children—Jesus came to his own people Israel
>dog—Greeks
>dogs under the table eat children's crumbs—give me your dregs: heal my daughter

Mark 7: 33–37 v 5: 1–20 Two ways of restoring In 10 cities (Decapolis)
deaf mute: finger in ear, spit finger on tongue—don't tell
demon possessed: command to demons—tell all

Motif: a recurring item in the story—bread
bread—physical, will feed 4000 or 5000
bread—spiritual, Jesus is bread of heaven
yeast of pharisees—hypocrisy, They want a sign, but none given to them
bread—hardness of heart; disciples forgot bread, discount their one loaf (see 4:35)

Chapter 8	Chapter 9	Chapter 10
blind death	death	death **blind**
given notice	notice	notice **given**
sight		**sight**

Children.................................. Servanthood
1. Millstone for bad guys   1. Say no to self
2. Jesus blessed them   2. Who is greatest among disciples,
                                                     a child
3. Kingdom of God like them   3. Request by James and John
                                              4. Service is #1

Question: How do demons come out? By Jesus or by demon allies?
Transformation
    To get eternal life
    Divorce, remarriage

Mark 9:42–47 Hyperbole—exaggeration to make a point

Mark 9: 1–8 Transformation/Transfiguration: Jesus shows his glory
1. Bright whiteness
2. Elijah and Moses represent prophets and Law
3. Peter's remark—build three shrines
4. Cloud, voice "My beloved Son—Listen to Him

    Temple Antics—Mark 12–13
I. Inside
    A. Teaching
        1. Parable—tenant farmers
        2. Temple—place for prayer
        3. Lord—David's Son?
        4. Widow contributes most
        5. Keep watch

Polly Riddle

    B. Testing
        1. Whose authority?
        2. Taxes—do we pay them?
        3. Whose wife?
        4. What's the greatest commandment?

II. Outside
    A. Beauty—big stones
    B. Fate—will be rubble

Jesus enters Jerusalem (Chapter 11)	Rome enters Jerusalem from other end*
on donkey	on horses
palm branches	spears
common people	Pilate, Herod, soldiers
blessing to David's son	Hail, King Caesar
Hosanna—Jesus is Lord	Caesar is Lord

    (*Teaching from a Lenten Lecture, 2011)

(Parable—one point; Allegory—many representations)
    Tenant farmers—Pharisees
    man/rich owner—God
    Vineyard—Israel
    Servants—Prophets
    Son—Jesus
Point: God's current help to be replaced

motif: fig tree
    leaves—hypocrisy, no fruit (if leaves, then fruit)
    withered—have faith in God
    tender branch—sign summer coming

Mark's Case for Jesus as God's Son

Baptism, Transformation—voice, Beloved Son
    Crucifixion—Centurion (15:39) surely God's Son
Authority—same as John's, recognized by Pharisees
    Not Satan—house divided cannot stand
Sins forgiven—Jesus heals paralyzed man
People amazed, awed, overwhelmed—Jesus does all things well: heals, casts out demons, feeds; wind and sea obey him; teaches with authority, not like scribes/legal experts
Pharisees, Saducees, Legal Experts—test Jesus but defeated
    They recognized themselves in parable of tenant farmers.
    15:32 (derisive) "Let the Christ, King of Jews, come down"
High Priest asks Jesus (14:61–2), "Are you the Christ, Son of the Blessed One?"
    Answer: I am (God is "I am who I am")
Pilate: recognized jealousy: formal charge—King of the Jews
Soldier-Surely this was the Son of God!

CPSIA information can be obtained at www.ICGtesting.com
Printed in the USA
BVOW05s1757130914

366655BV00002B/3/P